THE
INTEGRAL
NATURE OF THINGS

THE
INTEGRAL
NATURE OF THINGS

Critical Reflections on the Present

LATA MANI

LONDON NEW YORK NEW DELHI

First published 2013 in India
by Routledge
912 Tolstoy House, 15–17 Tolstoy Marg, Connaught Place,
New Delhi 110 001

Simultaneously published in the UK
by Routledge
4 Park Square, Milton Park, Abingdon, Oxon OX14 4RN

Routledge is an imprint of the Taylor & Francis Group, an informa business

Cover image: Untitled work by an anonymous artist, Jaipur, 2001, originally
published in Frank André Jamme, *Tantra Song: Tantric Painting from Rajasthan*
(Los Angeles: Siglio, 2011). Reproduced with the permission of the publisher.

Cover and book design by
Jackfruit Research & Design

Typeset by
Solution Graphics
A–14, Indira Puri,
Loni Road,
Ghaziabad, Uttar Pradesh 201 102

British Library Cataloguing-in-Publication Data
A catalogue record of this book is available from the British Library

ISBN: 978-0-415-83138-3

Contents

Acknowledgements

Writing the acknowledgements has, in many ways, been
the hardest part of completing this book. Yet this difficulty
dramatises the central issue I have sought to explore in
these pages: the interrelatedness of things and the challenge
of crafting a language and framework adequate to this
fact. How do I express gratitude for all that has inspired,
sustained and prompted me to put fingers to the keyboard?
Any reckoning would have to include music, birds, trees,
Bengalurean breezes, rain, food, friendships, meditation, and
last but not least academic, political and literary forbears and
contemporaries. But such a list would be partial. It would not
include the chance remark, gesture, or musical phrase that
initiated or crystallised the thought, feeling or intuition that
eventually found expression here. So let me just say a heartfelt
thank you to all that has enabled me to flourish, to all those
who (whether or not they know it) have been my companions
on this journey.

That said, I would like to thank those who shepherded this
manuscript at Routledge, New Delhi. And beyond, Annapurna
Garimella for designing the book in a way that enables the text
to breathe.

INTRODUCTION:
ONE DAY AT NOON

It was a bright August day. The light had a piercing quality, sharpened by the sun's refraction through clouds that hung thick and low. In the grassy field abutting my apartment, things were unfolding with their customarily relaxed precision. It was lunchtime; not just for me but for the goats as well. I was yet to discover where they spent their mornings. But at noon the herd would arrive to graze just where I, seated at my dining table, could see them. The goatherd would take her station under the English tamarind and knit or sew while the animals and I tucked into our respective repasts. Except at the height of summer they always came at this time. It was only my schedule that often required me to forgo this conviviality.

There was something comforting about the regularity of this ritual. Having noted their arrival I would put on some music, set the table and eat my meal, looking up occasionally, as one naturally does, to take in whatever is in one's line of vision.

On this day I was listening to *Ocean of Remembrance: Sufi Improvisations and Zikhrs*.[1] It had been recorded in the thick of a blizzard during Ramadan by the Turkish musician and psychiatrist, Oruç Güvenç. The pulsing stillness of the chanting filled the air.

Hearing the goatherd tap her stick on the ground with a particularly emphatic 'Hhey! Hhey!' I looked up. I was taken aback by what I saw. The goat was twirling. Goats are known to occasionally jump in a circular motion. But there was something different here, which is why the goatherd seemed to be disturbed. Unlike the usual awkwardness that characterises this motion, the goat was spinning gracefully. It seemed oblivious to its surroundings. As I walked toward the balcony to get a closer look I realised that the goat's movements were synchronous with the chanting. I stared in disbelief.

Meanwhile the goatherd seemed to be getting desperate. Perhaps it was the unusual nature of what was unfolding before her. Unable to stop the goat with her stern exhortations she started to beat the animal. But it was undeterred, as though it did not feel the impact of her increasingly violent blows.

The beauty of the chanting, the dancing goat, the consternation of the goatherd, the ensuing violence, the unperturbed grazing by the rest of the herd as though nothing were happening: it was surreal. And if this were not enough, into my consciousness at this time flowed unbidden the knowledge that the goat had, in a past life, been a whirling dervish. The vibration of the chanting had been irresistible to it. Past and present had fortuitously converged, bringing unexpected joy. 'If only the goatherd knew', I thought to myself, 'she would stop caning the animal!'

I watched as she gave up on her failed mission to stop the animal from behaving oddly. Minutes later the goat came slowly to a standstill. It stretched and then wandered off amiably into the rest of the herd, becoming undistinguishable from them to my untutored eye. The whole episode had lasted about five minutes. But it has stayed with me, raising questions for which I am still seeking answers.

II

On what basis do we decide what to do in a given situation? Is knowledge of what is happening a necessary prerequisite for knowing how to act? How do we respond when faced with something we do not understand? What did the goatherd's violence achieve? If we accept the fact that we cannot know everything, on what principles might we consider living our lives? How important is it for a reader to accept the story about the past life of the goat in order to continue reading this text? Is my conviction of its veracity best described as 'faith'? Can we see it as intimating a kind of knowing which, though many would reject, can pose questions other than those already familiar to us? What might we learn if we were to provisionally accept such 'knowing' for experiment's sake?

Whatever our view of reincarnation and whether the goat was in fact a sufi dancer in a previous life, we can agree that it seemed to be transported for a time and then without fuss returned to grazing with its companions. At the time I was chagrined that the goatherd had not been privy to the knowledge I had spontaneously received, for I felt it could have prevented her violent response. However, as I thought about it some more, it became clear to me that had the goatherd simply recognised the goat as an equal, as a being endowed with intelligence, she might have been startled, but not fearful. She may have found it easy to be patient, to be comfortable with not knowing what was going on. Rather than be overcome by panic, she may have been filled with curiosity. After all, no one was being harmed.

The episode dramatises a set of concerns that cut across this collection. The goatherd evinces an orientation to the world that is dominant in this time, one founded in a distrust of the unfamiliar and the inclination to dismiss or discipline anything that threatens some notion of order or appropriateness. Such a stance precludes a spacious relationship to phenomena. Knowledge — by extension life — comes to be construed as a set of procedures for containing and taming complexity, not as the expansive, mysterious, perplexing process of communing with all that surrounds us, one in which there are no foregone conclusions or guaranteed outcomes. The effort to impose our will, remake things in our preferred image of them, requires that we ignore, deny, repress and reconceive the multiplicitous and integral nature of things. Indifference to process and consequence inevitably follow. Can we then be surprised if the crisis we face today is multidimensional — cognitive, political, economic, cultural, ecological, above all, ethical?

III

It would not be considered radical to propose that the world is an interdependent singular whole of which everything is an integral, albeit complexly related, part. Yet the ways of thinking and being we have come to privilege tend to disaggregate self and phenomena from the multiple dimensions with which they are inextricably bound. This book traces contemporary aspects of this problem in a number of domains: language, labour, technology, post-structuralist theory, political rhetoric, urban planning and the cultural logic of neoliberal globalisation as witnessed from the so-called 'Silicon Valley of India', the city of Bengaluru. I am interested in how market-driven distillations of post-Enlightenment conceptions obscure the interrelations between persons, things, phenomena, aspects of self, humans and the rest of nature. The disarticulation of that which is integrally related inevitably leads to violence, miasma and, to use a Hindu-Buddhist term, *adharma* (that which violates equality, interdependence, interconnection, mutuality and reciprocity).

The essays that follow analyse the consequences of a variety of such disarticulations. In them I explore the prevailing and lapsed meanings of words, the rational and that which it excludes, the 'isness'[2] of things and the indivisibility of body, mind and heart in order to think through some of the limitations and losses in how we have come to understand the world.[3] My concern is to draw attention to the fact of misperception and to its sociocultural and political implications. But I am equally impelled by the way such misperception diminishes the rich potential of our experience, leading to the restlessness and discontent that we have come to take for granted as being intrinsic to humanness.

It is a regrettable fact that the human subdivision has in large measure refused to abide by the facts of interdependent mutuality whether in relation to itself or to the rest of nature. It has naturalised hierarchy and the right of some humans to dominate others on a variety of spurious grounds including class, caste, race, religion, gender, sexuality, ethnicity, ability.

In the modern period we have taken a similar view of nature. Viewing ourselves as a self-evidently higher species we have behaved as if the rest of nature exists only for our benefit and it is our right to exploit it as we please. Tribal communities have challenged this worldview and we have much to learn from them in this regard.

This work is grounded in the presumption that humans are one species among billions and not superior to any other; that all things have sentience, even those we generally regard as inanimate. Given the complexity of this reality it is not possible to know all of the interrelationships between all of the entities. The fantasy of omniscient knowledge or a comprehensive theory makes way for a modest and situated practice of sense-making. One learns to keep company with 'don't know'. It is partly in recognition of this that I have adopted a rhetorical strategy that interweaves observation, speculation and argument.

For most of what I argue in this book I can, and do, offer evidence. However, there are also things that I cannot substantiate, for example that the goat in a past life was indeed a whirling dervish. I cannot 'explain' how I received this information and though I could describe the process, it would not help any. And certainly I cannot convince anyone as to why they should trust this claim. Some of what follows is not science and from its perspective would fail to convince on counts of proof and replicability.

What then do we have here? Essays that take the recognisable form of sociocultural analysis, interspersed with observational accounts and philosophy in its root sense of wisdom for living. The book comprises short pieces: mostly prose, a few poems. It is structured so that the argument can accumulate density as core concerns are examined (and revisited) in a number of different contexts. The intermixing of genres is an attempt to convey sensory experience and the texture of things. In a period when opacity has come to characterise the grand abstractions of the ruling paradigm, it seemed to me that it may be the small stories, the textual pen and ink sketches of the everyday, that might, just might, loosen the hold of so-called settled truths. I hope readers will find the text open enough to admit a variety of entry points whether they ultimately reject what they encounter in its pages or find points of convergence with their own thinking.

Notes

1. Oruç Güvenç and Tümata, *Ocean of Remembrance: Sufi Improvisations and Zikhrs*, Interworld, B0000018D5, © 1995 Interworld Music.
2. 'Isness' is the specific quality and expression of sentience or 'aliveness' manifested by a person or thing.
3. In tracing the meanings of words I have used as references both *The Compact Oxford English Dictionary, Complete Text Reproduced Micrographically*, 2nd edn, New York: Oxford University Press, 1991; and *Webster's New Universal Unabridged Dictionary*, 2nd edn, New York: Simon and Schuster, 1983. The specific source is indicated whenever a word or entry is read closely.

THE AESTHETICS OF DISPLAY

Rolls of left-over cotton thread, locks and keys arranged by size and type, a giant *chappal* garlanded by miniature ones, plastic buckets donning mugs for caps.

Conical towers of *kumkum* and *gulal*, silvery-blue fish under a tarpaulin sky, plantain leaves rolled in multiples of fives, sentry-like cleavers, sickles and knives.

Chicken kebabs on vertical skewers, a rectangular mural of bras and panties, stainless steel sieves strung in circular formation, horizontal bins filled with ready-to-eat snacks.

Mallikarjun Katakol takes as his subject the aesthetics of display.[1] His images evoke a sensuous response. One is tempted to touch the objects in his photographs, feel the cool green of the betel leaf, ease out a slice from the pineapple tower, trace the pliable weave of stiff wicker baskets. The compositions are carefully crafted. A tender attentiveness characterises each arrangement and his images capture the loving tryst between merchant and merchandise. Katakol's photographs represent quotidian practices which many take for granted and few regard as art. The series invites us to re-examine the terms 'art', 'aesthetics', and 'display'.

II

The history of the words 'art' and 'aesthetics' is interwoven. 'Art', from the Latin word, *artem*, means 'skill'. Like any word its scope has varied across the centuries. Today 'art' has come to be associated almost entirely with the work of those skilled in painting, drawing, sculpture, photography, and new media. But this was not always the case. If one traces the European trajectory of the term, we would discover that art in the medieval period included grammar, logic, arithmetic, music and astronomy. The skills we now consider as art only began to be affiliated with it in the late 17th century and it was only in the late 19th century that their dominant association with the term was fully secured. In order for this to take place, art had to be distinguished as a specific kind of skill, one practised to a particular end. It was in this process that a general term became particularised and a number of other words increasingly bore the semantic weight of what was now excluded by it.[2]

The most potent example of this is perhaps the distinction between 'artist' and 'artisan' or 'craftsperson'. The former is deemed to use his or her skills in a uniquely personal way to an imaginative end. The latter is held to draw on inherited tradition and convention for a utilitarian purpose. While this does not imply that art is never purposive nor draws upon tradition or that artisanal or craft productions never reflect imagination and an individual impress, a hierarchy has come to characterise the relationship between these terms. This fact is reflected in the different social value attributed to each: the artist is considered to be superior to the artisan with his or her work explicitly defined as art, not craft.

This development is characterised by two simultaneous processes. First, a hierarchy of practices is created out of what was previously conceived of as a diversity of skills. Second, this hierarchy depends on extracting these skills from their integral relationship to everyday practices and relocating them in a distinct realm of specialisation. This is not to say that prior to this there were no specialists, for there were indeed persons dedicated to specific practices. This process of reordering was not about clarifying competencies within a skill set, namely, distinguishing the amateurs from the experts. It was rather about conceptually separating skills from their relationship to quotidian life practices and resituating them in a cognitive and symbolic register indifferent to their embeddedness in the everyday. Art then becomes the provenance of specialists who undertake their practice in an allegedly distinct sphere. And those same skills when evidenced in myriad daily practices are no longer considered art.

A similar process may be traced in the history of the word 'aesthetics'. 'Aesthetics' is derived from the Greek word, *aesthesis*, meaning 'pertaining to ... things perceptible by the senses'.[3] It refers to things that are material as opposed to things that are thinkable or immaterial. The *Oxford English Dictionary* states that this meaning of the term is now obsolete, for since the mid-19th century the word has predominantly come to mean 'of or pertaining to the appreciation or criticism of the beautiful'.[4] Aesthetics is now firmly associated with taste, refinement, beauty, with visual appearance and the arts. The older meaning of the term still lingers amongst us in our use of the word 'anaesthetic' to signify the absence of the capacity for sense perception. This, as Raymond Williams points out, has ruled out 'anaesthetic' as the negative of 'aesthetic' and led to our using 'unaesthetic' or 'nonaesthetic' instead.[5]

We have here a significant transformation. Aesthetics goes from having to do with sense perception of the thing itself, to being about the perceiver's capacity to discern the beautiful or refined. Aesthetics is no longer the perception of an object by the senses; rather objects are considered aesthetic according to whether they conform to some standard of taste or beauty. In this way of thinking, beauty and sensuousness are not inherent properties of things in themselves but the effect of things being agreeable to some convention regarding them. From a term that could have applied to every object in the phenomenal world that our senses apprehend, aesthetics is narrowed such that only certain things qualify. This parallels the mutation and constriction of 'art' and is, not surprisingly, a contemporaneous process.

'Display' is the third in the triumvirate of terms that relates to our contemplation of Katakol's photographs. Display has two linked but distinct dimensions, one tending toward the descriptive and another toward the evaluative. The former is evident when 'display' as verb is defined as unfolding or exposing to view, making manifest, causing to be observed. The evaluative aspect is brought to the fore when 'display' is used to reference ostentatious exhibition or making a show of something. It can be argued that these two meanings of 'display' echo the transformations in the terms 'art' and 'aesthetics' outlined previously. 'Display' as manifestation tends toward an earlier definition of 'art' as 'skill' and of 'aesthetics' as 'sense perception of material phenomena'. By contrast, display as making a show of something is more consonant with a notion of art as the skill of the specialist and aesthetics as evincing specific notions of beauty and taste considered to be refined. After all, artists make a show of their work in exhibitions while vendors display their wares in order to bring it to the view of potential customers. The fact that displays are also exhibits and that artists are also seeking customers for their work simply underlines the artificial nature of the hierarchy between what is and is not considered art and who is and is not regarded an artist.

A few caveats are in order. As concepts 'art' and 'aesthetics' have been extensively debated by philosophers, artists and art historians. Such contests are not traceable through dictionary definitions. The thesaurus does, however, help us delineate transformations in the popular meaning of a given word. Second, the European history of terms cannot simply be transposed to the Indian context. There is a substantial and rich Indian literature on aesthetics and in the past century the *rasa* theory, for example, has been extended to address the visual arts.[6] Third, the semantic shifts we have noted here are integral to the transition to modernity in Europe. Modernity in India is still a work in progress marked by ongoing battles and negotiated truces between multiple ways of seeing. Victories as well as losses are frequently temporary and the victors are not always those who are allied with power or modernity. For instance, the jury is still out as to whether malls will ultimately displace the traditional shop and bazaar even in urban areas.

Nevertheless, a case can be made regarding the relevance of this discussion to our current context. The *rasa* theory proposes its own hierarchy by distinguishing between appropriate and inappropriate or spurious rasas. This is the broader civilisational context in which our cultural practices can be seen to simultaneously honour and dishonour matter, to embrace phenomena in their totality at one moment only to reject this principle in the next. This has consequences similar to that noted above in context of the transition to modernity in Europe when aesthetics as a holistic apprehension of phenomena is fragmented and reordered along an axis that is hierarchical and exclusionary. Our ambivalence to matter and the phenomenal world forms the backdrop to our encounter with modernity's evaluative schema. It cannot surprise us if we have come to use art and aesthetics in a way that reflects the European sense of these terms even if the route of our arrival was a different one.

III

Mallikarjun Katakol's display series is shot in contemporary Bengaluru although these pictures could just as easily have been taken in any other Indian city. The photographs are of goods for sale: vegetables, meat, fish, dry goods, snacks, vessels, footwear, accessories, undergarments, locks, etc. The images yield very little of their context. What we have are representations of objects. Even though the advertising and display of commodities leads the charge in generating sensory overload in urban settings today, the images are refreshing.

The arrangement of items is traditional even as form appears to follow function reflecting a design principle considered modern. Things are set out in a manner that presupposes a mixture of self-service and the need for assistance. The way things are placed — piled, hung, stacked, strung together — is reminiscent of the bazaar and its aesthetic which still remains our preferred experience of shopping, notwithstanding the retail outlets and malls that have mushroomed in Indian cities. The bazaar signifies variety, plenitude and a joyful commingling of things that are related by no other principle than that of contiguity (the fact of being next to each other). This is the adventure of being at a traditional market. Even though the photographs are close-ups of particular items, they manage to evoke this broader context.

Katakol meticulously observes the composition of each display, its colour, texture, symmetry, detail and patterning. He directs our gaze to the curvature of *kadais*, the play of shape and colour in the way the vegetable vendor sets out her produce or the *masala* merchant his spices. His images extend the aesthetic of the original display. It is as if his camera is poised between the item and the hurried gaze of the city dweller whose life circumstances can lead him or her to barely notice the quiet aesthetics of traditional practices that overwhelmingly predominate, and yet remain symbolically marginal to the city's sense of itself as modern. His images manifest the same care as the displays he has photographed. To honour subjects/objects in this way is to temporally and culturally situate the photographer alongside them and not to position him or her as apart and/or superior. This is evident in the photograph of underwear which would more commonly have been treated as kitsch. Instead our attention is drawn to how the display resembles appliqué work or is suggestive of a network of urban clothes-lines fluttering with bras and panties.

The photograph of slaughtered goats in a mutton shop perhaps best expresses Katakol's approach. Headless and hung from its knee joints we see the goat's torso: backbone, ribs, blood. In anyone else's hands it could have been a disturbing image. Instead, we have a representation in which the fact of slaughter, the skill of the work of slaughter and the beauty of the animal converge to confront the viewer. The non-judgemental directness of the image suggests that the photographer neither intends to shock the viewer nor protect her or him. We are prompted to reflect on what we behold. In context of an urbanism that invites us to shrink-wrap and plastic-coat our relationship to our environment the evocation of such a response is welcome.

Katakol's photographs are premised on the inseparability of life and art. They help us recall the skills that have traditionally made life sensuous in the Indian cultural setting and to which many today are indifferent. His photographs remind us that art is not merely about the ability to *do* something to matter, a tendency that has led to the privileging of certain kinds of practices and of formal experimentation per se. Art is equally about celebrating matter and the many modes of communing with it. It can enable us to see, hear, feel, touch and smell things in and as themselves, to fully experience our capacity for sense perception. Mallikarjun Katakol's display series exemplifies this vital function of art.

Notes

1. Inaugural talk presented at Mallikarjun Katakol's Photography Exhibit, 'The Aesthetics of Display', Goethe Institute/Max Mueller Bhavan, 17 April 2009. The photographs may be viewed at http://www.mallikarjunkatakol. com (accessed 6 June 2012).

2. Raymond Williams, 'Aesthetic', in *Keywords: A Vocabulary of Culture and Society*, London: Fontana/Croon Helm, 1976, pp. 27–28.
3. *The Compact Oxford English Dictionary, Complete Text Reproduced Micrographically*, 2nd edn, New York: Oxford University Press, 1991, p. 206.
4. Ibid.
5. Williams, 'Aesthetic', p. 27.
6. K. G. Subramanyan, 'Visual Arts and the Concept of Rasa', in *The Magic of Making: Essays on Art and Culture*, Calcutta: Seagull, 2007, pp. 77–90.

THE GRASS CUTTER

Our life is not merely shaped by the people we know. It is equally formed by those we see regularly but do not know. Such individuals may be an even more intimate part of our days than those we consider to be close friends. We may set our watch by them. Or deem their appearance or non-appearance a kind of arbiter of our day, the sign of things to come. The grass cutter is one such person.

For the past seven years I have seen him walking back and forth carrying loads whose weight and proportion should (in my view at least) topple and bury him. But no. He is a master of what he does.

I should have known from the way he carries his sickle. It is either tucked under his arm like a question mark on its side, or else hangs playfully from the palm of his hand. He walks with the swaying gait of a classical dancer on stage. The particular harmony of masculine strength and feminine grace that he manifests is beautiful to behold.

I have learned he is married and has three adult children who ignore him. That he considers the grass to be his Goddess Lakshmi. That She has enabled him to get four sisters married and provide for his own family. That on Mondays he starts work only after participating in the Shiva *puja* at the temple on the edge of the lakebed. I learned all of this from a friend who struck up a conversation with him one morning. He also told her that he loved his work. This did not surprise me.

I have never spoken to him although we did cross paths once. I was startled when I saw his familiar frame coming toward me. I was used to seeing him in profile from the second floor, and here we were about to be face-to-face at ground level. I stood to the side and let him pass noticing that his nose was flatter than I had believed and his eyes set wider apart.

He and I do have a language in common — Tamil. But what could I have said? 'I am so glad to meet you! You have no idea how important you are in my life. I feel happy when I see you first thing in the morning. And do you know that if I am concerned about something, and happen to look out and see you there, I feel it is a sign that things will turn out well?!'

He would have thought me mad and I could not have blamed him. And yet, every word of such an outburst would have been true. We matter to each other in ways we may never know. We bring joy by our presence, our very beingness.

Our sense of affinity exceeds the categories we are accustomed to using in seeking to understand our relationships with each other. True, the grass cutter and I have no 'relationship' if by that is meant conscious interaction, one inevitably mediated by the differences in our relative economic positions and social ascriptions (class, caste, gender, sexuality, among others). But within, and beyond, and before all of this is the fact of our connectedness as energy and 'isness', forms of existence to which any notion of hierarchy is irrelevant. A conceptual framework that cannot admit this a priori and make room for its implications does not serve us well.

Is this why Left and feminist arguments can at times reify the very categories that they have painstakingly demonstrated to be social constructions? Somewhere along the way we have begun to treat as complete and self-evident what we ourselves have claimed to be partial and contingent descriptions. People collapse into their social identities; appear to be contained by them. Depending on how it is crafted, identity politics can lend weight to such compressed representations. It is as if the differences that particularise us have all but overwhelmed our presumption of the equality that binds us.

When concern about difference consistently outweighs embrace of our fundamental commonality we belittle who we are and could be to each other. We begin to see each other as the dominant order would like us to. Merely inverting the paradigm or swapping margin and centre does little on its own. We are in dire need of a new way of thinking about the interweaving of difference, sameness, distinction, mutuality and socially-produced hierarchy.

It is likely that the grass cutter will never know his significance in my life. Nor will others with whom I experience a similar sense of kinship. I do not wish otherwise. More important to me than whether they know is the fact that it is simply by being as they are that they bless my life. It is wonderful to learn that being ourselves is as much of a gift to others as anything we may do for them.

AVENUE ROAD SUITE

EVERY ASPECT A WORLD UNTO ITSELF

Densely-packed, labyrinthine streets are lined with higgledy-piggledy constructions. Lean blocks rise skyward beside squat single-storey buildings framed by clouds. Shops have sprung up on every step and along each wall. A young man makes and sells jewellery under the overhang of an air conditioner. Others sit huddled between the vertical stacks of books that line the walkways. The nut seller, a regular fixture at the mouth of one of the area's many *gullies*, inspects his display as he awaits a customer.

One might presume that these outdoor sellers are itinerant salesmen. But some have been here for as long as 60 years! Every inch of pavement (sidewalk), every step, corner and crevice hosts some commercial enterprise. Avenue Road is the city's wholesale market. It is said to be the smallest area with the largest volume of financial transactions in Asia. It is the hub from which Bengaluru grew.

People and goods snake their way in and out of lanes that radiate in all directions. Handcarts, trolleys, *tempos*, two-wheelers weighted down in front and back: every conceivable means of ferrying goods may be seen here. Men and women expertly balance loads on their heads, carry long steel rods between them, or roll cables coiled like ferris-wheels alongside the curb.

A wide variety of people may be seen jostling each other: old men in turbans, young girls in *salwar kameez*, men in jeans, women in trousers or sarees. Bell bottoms, *dhotis*, pyjama *kurtas*, shorts: in any half hour the history and present of fashion unfolds before one. Everyone except the urban upper middle class comes to Avenue Road.

Shops occupy the ground floor of buildings. Offices and homes are most often to be found on the floors above. As one steps into the dark and musty entrances to climb the invariably rickety stairs, the noise of the street quickly falls away. It is as if one is entering another space and time. How is it that the energy and bustle of the street does not intrude into the interior of these buildings?

Past and present coexist in amiable, unselfconscious contiguity. Art deco, lattice wood-work and tube lights are neighbours with glass facades, plastic cladding and recessed tungsten bulbs. The homes at the rear of shop fronts or on the floors above them retain many original early 20th-century features: iron beams from Middlesbrough, United Kingdom (UK), rosewood panels, brass light switches. Often, the only evident break with the past is the decision to use a single colour in painting the interior; multiple and contrasting shades were earlier used to highlight the careful detailing.

No single aesthetic dominates. Both inside and outside exemplify an exuberant and casual mix of old and new. Such promiscuity may be offensive to one who longs for the coherence and order of an integrated sensibility. But it is this diversity that gives Avenue Road its particular charm.

There is no place from which to get a bird's eye view, a sense of this area in its entirety. It can be experienced only in the density of its details: the temple, the shoe seller, the flower vendor, the *jalebi-wallah*, the jeweller, the textile showroom, the stationery kiosk, the *shambrani* swirling as the young man from the mosque undertakes his daily round of blessing. Every aspect is a world unto itself, many-layered and richly engrossing.

Avenue Road is akin to a river; to experience it one must be willing to be part of its flow, even if only temporarily. There is no way to stand apart, to look from a distance, or look down from above at the teeming activity below. One cannot relate to it from the sequestered comfort of one's car. The only option is to walk its streets.

The city is planning to widen Avenue Road. A straight line is expected to cut a swath across the maze of lanes, flattening buildings and scattering people and businesses to some other, as yet undisclosed, location. What will be the repercussions of destroying structures that lean into and against each other on all fronts? Thousands will be displaced.

To those in favour of this plan it is a small price to pay for transforming Bengaluru into a 'global city'. To those critical of this approach to urban development no sacrifice is worth the destruction of life worlds that will necessarily follow. Residents and businesses on Avenue Road are divided on the issue. Some would prefer to move to a modern location. They sense that the new elite of young and well-paid professionals are reluctant to wander its by-lanes and that in the years to come other shoppers may feel likewise. Their commercial interests outweigh any particular affection for their current location. Others propose shifting the wholesale businesses elsewhere so that the retail shops can continue to operate in a less-crowded milieu.

Even as practical solutions are debated, a key cultural and existential issue remains unexplored: what are the consequences of substituting the multiplicity of logics that comprise the ecosystem of Avenue Road today, with the singular and hierarchical paradigm that underwrites the dominant approach to urban development, one that treats all perspectives other than its own as outdated and in need of revision?

The question is not based on a nostalgic desire for the old or a suspicion of modernity per se. There is much room for improvement of the physical space and infrastructure for those who live, work or shop on Avenue Road. Furthermore, it is a known fact that caste and religious tensions interweave the interdependencies that characterise lives and livelihoods here. This is no utopian space.

Notwithstanding this, the prevailing ethos accepts diversity as an organising principle of life activity and implicitly honours cooperation and interdependence as necessary virtues. These core values are expressed in the way people and businesses function today. Shops permit pavement vendors to store merchandise on their premises at the end of each day. Traditional practices of alms giving and receiving are part of the daily routine. A moral economy of reciprocity is evident. Is this why there is no frenzy on the street despite the large numbers of people, goods and vehicles that traverse it each day?

The push to create global cities (the current face of modernity in the realm of urban planning) brings an altogether different perspective to bear on the social organisation of space. It conceives of roads as transit passages. Motorised vehicles are privileged over all other modes of transportation while pedestrians have virtually no rights despite outnumbering all other road users. This framework also has unambiguous views on what constitutes legitimate street activity. Pavement vendors and hawkers whose right to exist is presently nurtured will instantly become trespassers to be evicted. An interdependent community will be disaggregated into those who own property and those who don't.

Avenue Road as it presently exists cannot survive the implementation of road widening. Its world defies that of the modernisers of today. Though hierarchical, it is an accommodative space in which the interests of many are taken into account at least to some degree. Avenue Road evinces much of what modernity celebrates: economic enterprise, ingenuity, commercial success. But it does so in a manner that conjoins social hierarchy and entitlement with notions of social obligation that include recognition of interdependence and a multiplicity of needs. As a result it sets aside two virtues dear to modernity: individualism and self-sufficiency. History as well as current events suggest that this may not necessarily be a bad thing.

THE TREE

The bustle of the street keeps one's eye on the ground. It
is easy to walk past the tree noticing nothing other than
its canopy of green leaves: a welcome relief to the built
environment that dominates all else. But should one pause
and look up one beholds something unusual: the tree appears
to have grown out of the building.

The trunk hugs the outer wall. Its branches arch over the
pavement. A few roots may be seen disappearing into the
brick. There is no tree stump anchoring it to the earth; no
visible place inaugurating its subterranean form as a network
of roots. It is as if the mature tree were an air plant.

'Air plant' is the common name for epiphytes. Epiphytes
are plants that do not root in the soil. They grow upon
another plant or building. They rely on their hosts only
for physical support. Nutrition is provided by air, rain,
photosynthesis. Although not parasites, they can at times
damage their hosts. Moss, lichen and bromeliads are well
known epiphytes.

This tree may be likened to an epiphyte but it certainly cannot be considered one. A tree depends on being rooted in the earth for its existence. Somewhere between and beneath the brick and concrete are roots that draw their sustenance from the soil. Have they gone deeper than the foundation of the three-storey building? Or have they grown in a lateral direction to ensure their survival?

The relationship of tree and building epitomises an essential dimension of life on Avenue Road. Each has allowed the other to exist. The tree could have been felled. Instead it has been permitted to grow on the building's façade. But little else seems to have been done to nurture it. Its base lies entombed beneath the concreted pavement away from any direct sun, air, moisture.

The only trees that remain fully-standing in the area are those around whose base temples have been built. And here too, with signal exceptions, one sees only the branches some 20 to 30 feet above ground. The trunk and base are hidden from view, accessed only by entering the temple itself. From the street it would seem that these too are epiphytes.

Sanctifying some trees while neglecting others is so common that it does not evoke irony. Our attitude evinces a hierarchy that does not exist in the natural world. Still, the trees offer the cool of their green without reluctance. Their vitality in these conditions is a mystery that uplifts.

THE ROOM

Brother and sister live atop a flight of stairs that is in complete disrepair. A 10-foot-by-10-foot room doubles as a living-cum-sleeping area. To its right is a tiny enclosure that is the kitchen. Neither bathroom nor toilet are in evidence; they are presumably to be found off the dark corridor to the right of the entry door and shared with others on the same floor. It is hard to believe that their grandfather once owned many of the properties on this narrow street that abuts Avenue Road.

The room is gaily cluttered. Photographs, calendars and wall hangings festoon every inch of available space. Elders, youngsters, gods, goddesses, certificates and plaques are nailed to the wall or neatly placed on the shelves that line it. A rope is strung across the room like an aerial bridge. On it hangs what is left of an old curtain made of wooden beads and clothes in need of airing. Beneath it, a fish tank filled with utilitarian and ornamental items serves as a curio cabinet. It would seem that every object ever bought or received has been retained and given a place.

Although the room is small and the objects many, one does not feel overwhelmed. A quiet dignity pervades the space. The objects seem to exist in and as themselves. They do not appear to carry the burden of family history or memory. They are not a mirror in which the past is sought or in which the present is reflected. They are found objects in the journey of life whose value is quietly acknowledged in their retention. Over time they have become integral to the lives that unfold in their midst: keepsakes that bear witness and offer a kind of joyful, silent companionship.

It is this relationship with objects that offers a clue to their arrangement. A *laissez-faire* approach is in evidence. Metal, plastic, cloth, wooden and paper items spanning four decades of production mingle in the fish tank. The television is perched between a statue and a stainless steel container. Its screen is visible only up close, being partially obscured by the curtain drooping from the clothes-line. An economy of space may be said to be at work. But it cannot by itself make sense of the artful jumble of things.

The aesthetic expresses a way of relating to artefacts in which the value of things has not been reduced to their function or to their sociocultural significance. This explains why there is no attempt to group items according to any consistent logic or to showcase a few so as to tacitly reflect some hierarchy, whether about the relative value of things or the status and imagined trajectory of those who possess them. Thus it is that the past does not hang heavily over the room and the future is nowhere to be found.

Not burdened by the weight of social attribution, the things in the room can be as they are. Our interest is evoked but without the accompanying anxiety that by and large mediates our current relationship to things in which humans and their belongings seemingly exist to prop each other up. These are simply objects one has gathered along the way and that one has chosen to keep. Owner and object are thus free to be in the present, as is the visitor. So it is that we feel spaciousness amidst the clutter. And the freedom to encounter the scene without past or future remaking what is before us.

THE STATIONERY STORE

Parvathiamma's store is right on Avenue Road. It is small:
5 feet wide and 7 feet deep. A short-statured woman she
sits perched on a high stool to the right of the rectangular
storefront next to the wall-mounted public phone. Outside,
the flow of people and vehicles continues all day long.

Before her husband's demise in 1990 Parvathiamma had
assisted him. She had handled customers while he had done
all the work that required leaving the store. The suppliers now
deliver directly so she can run her business without difficulty.
The store has been at that location for 25 years.

It is cool inside the rather cramped place even though there
is no cross ventilation and such opening as there is festooned
with school bags and other items for sale. A tubelight
hangs over the counter at the front while the rear is lit by
a fluorescent bulb dangling from the low ceiling. It is dark
enough inside for her to switch it on when she needs to look
for something in the back.

A steady stream of customers keeps her busy through most of
the day. Finding time to have an uninterrupted lunch can be

a challenge. On this afternoon there are many students; exams are approaching and they have come to buy pens, pencils, rulers, erasers, compasses, geometry sets.

She seems to know many customers by name. Some are from the neighbourhood. Others have come from afar. 'Not that they cannot buy these items elsewhere', she explains, 'but they have been coming to my store for years'. She is 'Aunty' to them all. Several pick up things with the promise to pay later. 'They are not strangers. Where will they go! Won't I be here to remind them when they next walk past?'

We converse in fits and starts as we are continually interrupted by customers. I am grateful as it gives me time to take in my surroundings. I ask her what she likes most about her job. She does not need to think. 'Being part of so many people's lives', she says smiling.

Parvathiamma feels safe running her store as a single woman. Almost all businesses on the street have been there for decades. People watch out for each other. 'When I don't come people worry', she says with quiet pride. Why then has there been no success in organising merchants against the prospect of road widening? She shrugs her shoulders. 'Each person wants something different. Some people feel they can move to a better location. I will close down my shop. There is no other option for me'.

A middle-aged man arrives to buy a ballpoint pen. He asks for one that takes refills. He confesses that the thought of throwing things away really upsets him. She commiserates but doesn't have any for sale. He walks on. 'See, he wants to reuse but many want to throw things away. It's like that with Avenue Road also'. She seems philosophical in the face of uncertainty. She is a small trader after all. Not knowing when she will be asked to vacate, she has started stocking only limited supplies. Her story illustrates the web of solidarity and each-to-his-own that characterises life on this street.

A STREET IS NOT A ROAD

A street is not a road. True, they are synonyms. But 'street'
evokes much more. Roads connect points in space. They are
moving corridors. Metalled, unmetalled, raised, sunken, pot-
holed, mud-packed, gravel-laden thoroughfares.

Streets are life worlds. People in action, cultures in play.
The street is a theatre of contiguity, chance, conflict, and
conviviality. A delicate, imprecise equilibrium.

The broader semantic range of 'street' is evident in our
language. 'Street smart', 'the Arab street' and 'the man on
the street' express how the street is a site of sociocultural
negotiation and political expression. While 'Dalal Street',
'Main Street', and 'Wall Street' are examples of named
locations that symbolise ideas even more than specific
geographical coordinates. By contrast, 'one for the road',
'hit the road' or 'road movie' retain the relation of 'road' to
journeying, to the process of moving through.

So it is that while 'boulevard', 'way', 'route', 'path', 'avenue',
'lane' or 'drive' may suffice as alternatives to either word

there are others that apply to 'street' alone. And these have to do with its meaning as cohabited space: residents, locals, occupants, dwellers, neighbourhood.

The tension between road and street is manifest in how widening a road can actually narrow a street in this broader sense. Street life is in inverse proportion to road width. Its vitality depends on either side of a road being within earshot of one another: on people, sound and activity traversing back and forth with ease. Two halves of a whole in fluid embrace.

This requires that a road be imagined in relation to the community it embeds: one axis among others in a living quadrant. Not merely as a conduit to and from privileged destinations.

When roads are not conceived as streets, they trespass. They encroach upon and infringe the variegated rhythms of life. Its diagonals, zigzags and recursive loops; its alternatingly casual, purposeful, meandering character. Its improvisational nature.

The road becomes a border. Slicing through neighbourhoods, hemming in segments, reconfiguring localities. Reminding us of the relation of 'road' to 'raid': hostile incursion against person or district, foray. This meaning of 'road' common in the 16th century is obsolete in the 20th. But its sense lingers in our use of the word 'inroad'. And in our experience of the consequences of city planning that focuses not on streets but on roads.

THE IDEAL OF A GLOBAL CITY

The concerted effort to create global cities out of our sprawling conurbations has pitted two logics against each other. Our cities have evolved over time. They have accommodated existing social relationships with their hierarchies and tensions and even managed, at times, to gradually modulate their impact on the lives of residents. Cities have grown by a relatively organic (though not benign) process of adaptation, flexibility, accretion.

People have been central to this story. Cold anonymity has not been a feature of our urbanism. Even in dire accounts of city life in India human succour has been present. It is people who have dynamised our streets. Still, as with Avenue Road, it has been a case of permitting coexistence without creating the conditions in which all can thrive. This explains the physical state of our cities, the challenges of the urban poor and our scant regard for nature, including the very trees that we need to continue breathing.

The global city is grounded in a different premise. It is obsessed with spatiality and appearance. For better as well as for worse, Indian cities have thus far tended to emphasise people over the spaces in which they live and work (prioritise would be too strong a term given the woeful conditions in which people have had to live). By contrast the so-called global city is an ideal that has little to do with the existing conditions of urban life in India. Its success would require not just the disappearance of structures but of the people that currently live, work, love and dream in and around them.

Our social ecology comprises a complex set of interdependencies that cannot be willed away. The present is not merely a staging ground for a desired future. The facts that constitute it cannot be ignored. The vision of a city of malls and skyscrapers, chrome and glass, whose streets are empty of people is illusory. There is no room in it for the majority. In any case, as many have pointed out, it overlooks the reliance on domestic and other help of the class whose fantasy it represents. The demand for a proximate labour pool will likely ensure that the streets remain lively though perhaps treacherous to use given the interloper status increasingly ascribed to pedestrians.

The choice cannot be between traditional areas filled with people and warmth but short on facilities, and an urban redevelopment which privatises and disciplines public space depriving most citizens of access to the commons. This would be to substitute one form of indifference for another. An approach that de facto privileges a small segment of society and criminalises the majority is even more regressive than the current attitude of 'live and let subsist' which has done little to enable the majority to flourish.

The conflict is not between those for and against development but between those willing to confront the economic, demographic, social, cultural and ecological facts and those who are not. This latter group, which includes a wide cross section of the intelligentsia in the government and the corporate sector, is in the thrall of an abstraction called 'the global city'. And it is prepared to pursue it relentlessly. It is thus that any dialogue promptly dissembles to reveal an ideological divide impervious to evidence and reason.

Not surprising then that urban planning has become a carnivalesque disregard of reality: road medians that need to be scaled, flyovers built within a whisker of buildings, the privileging of private over public transportation, the absence of planning for the thousands displaced by this quest for a city that looks a certain way.

The road widening plan for Avenue Road is a case in point. Even prior to the issue of rehabilitation is the following question: how practical is it to demolish buildings on either side of a main street in this rabbit warren-like area when the likelihood of taking down adjoining structures at their rear is a virtual given? The plan to widen, it seems, is concerned only with creating a broad road and not with its feasibility or consequences.

The divisions that have characterised our society, caste, gender, and at times religion, have been reflected in the spatial organisation of our cities and towns. It is a thoroughly inequitable order but it has until now recognised interdependency. In particular, caste and gender as hierarchical systems have actively required those deemed 'the other' in order to function at all. Social hierarchy and spatial proximity have accordingly been intrinsic features of urban life.

The elite of today equally depend on the labour of the poor and working classes. Yet, so taken are many by a certain conception of what makes a global city that they have begun to act as if what exists does not. Thus, a city teeming with people can be imagined as a network of pipes, drains, power cables, traffic corridors, cell phone towers, metro stations and ring roads (peripheral and inner) that lead to and from a mythical area called the central business district which is frequently not the commercial hub.

In a similar vein, trees become 'green cover' or 'lung spaces', seen to add colour or to function as a back-up respiratory system for humans, with no life of their own. And lakes are dubbed 'water bodies', a term that occludes their being home to fish, birds, lotuses, lilies and reeds. Encroachment of lakes is surreptitiously permitted and in due course regularised, even while a select few are handed over to private players to be dredged, cleaned and developed for use by those who can afford to pay.

The state of a city's infrastructure is considered key to its claim to being global. Infrastructure refers to 'the substructure or underlying foundation'. It has come to mean a city's civic amenities: roads, power, drains, water, sanitation, transportation. This conception inverts the real basis of a city; its *raison d'être*. Cities are places where *people* have gathered in substantial numbers to work and live. Amenities merely address the collective needs of inhabitants. The real foundation of any city is its people. One connotation of substructure is 'that which holds something together'. If one were to identify such an underlying principle in city life it would surely be interdependence. Work and life are inherently cooperative processes. Planning that is not premised on the reality of interdependent collaboration, and development that does not integrate it in every aspect of design and implementation, stands little chance of succeeding in the long term.

Any conception of 'the global city' that is at odds with the prevailing nature of Indian urbanism is equally at odds with its cultural substructure, a fact of far greater consequence. The global city proposes its own notions of space and time, promotes its own forms of consumption, its own 'lifestyle'. It is thus more than an economic and political force. It challenges entire ways of life (aesthetic practices, modes of being and forms of interpersonal and social relating). Not all such changes are unwelcome. But social dislocation and cultural alienation are as integral to the processes unleashed in its name as the promise of greater freedom and opportunity. To be wedded in this context to an ideal indifferent to facts, one that symbolically and literally excises the majority from the imagined future of our cities, is surely equivalent to destabilising the ground beneath our feet.

Note

* Fragments of 'Avenue Road Suite' were published as 'Urban Triptych', in Curt Gambetta and Ritajyoti Bandyopadhyay (eds), *The Future of the Street*, *Seminar*, August 2012, pp. 28–31.

THE MARKET IS LIKE THAT
BECAUSE PEOPLE ARE LIKE THIS

In *Keywords*, Raymond Williams ends his entry on 'Humanity', with the observation that in the mid-20th century, the term 'human' is used to denote 'what might be called condoned fallibility'.[1] Continuing, he states: '"He had a human side to him after all" need not mean only that some respected man was fallible; it can mean also that he was confused or, in some uses, that he committed various acts of meanness, deceit or even crime . . . [A]cts which would formerly have been described . . . as proofs of the faults of humanity are now adduced, with a sense of approval that is not always either wry or covert, as proof of being human (and likable is not usually far away)'.[2]

To Williams, the shift of perception represented by the emergence of the triad 'human-fallible-likable' was striking. 'Human' had always been understood as distinct from 'Divine' and there was a long history of conceding mortal imperfections ('to err is human'). What was new by the

1950s, however, was the increasingly positive evaluation of that which had previously been humanity's Achilles' heel. Today, this view has become so thoroughly normative that it would be unlikely to elicit remark. To Williams this transition characterised 'late bourgeois society'. In India the shift may be traced to neoliberalism and is evident where its cultural impact has been most intimately felt.

A new conventionalism holds sway. The uncritical veneration of power, sex and success (itself a triad). Edgy as hip. Bigger and faster as better. The valorisation of indulgence, obsession, desire. The notion that there is no such thing as too much. Alongside these new norms is a naturalisation of the anger, jealousy, competitiveness, aggression, humiliation, fear, insecurity and stress frequently experienced in attempting to pursue these ideals. To be sure these mindstates are natural in the sense that they are commonly experienced. What is different in the current period is that they have become explanatory logics unto themselves. By a sleight of hand the immediate context for this view of human nature, the market fundamentalism of neoliberalism, has come to be understood as its consequence. Put simply, 'The market is like that because people are like this'.

There is a long history of positing humans as selfish, aggressive, insecure and riven with desire of one kind or another. In Europe, for example, Christian philosophers, Enlightenment political theorists and, more recently, sociobiologists have all drawn upon these ideas in specific ways to different ends. In the Indian context, Hinduism and Buddhism have also addressed these aspects of humanness in arguing for the need to understand and tame the ego. But where religious philosophers emphasised these elements in order to propose ways to alleviate the suffering caused by them, and secular theorists proposed political structures to limit their negative social effects, the current market-derived paradigm simply offers itself as a rational means of satiating these tendencies of human nature. The role of the market in creating needs or the profit it derives from exploiting fear, insecurity or desire is in this process evaded.

It is true that this belief about markets and human nature can only persist so long as we collectively subscribe to it. We can withdraw our participation at any time that we choose. After all there is no gun to our heads. We can refuse to buy more than we need and reject the notion that excitement is the pursuit of desire, and freedom the ability to satisfy it. But many of us are in the thrall of the market and its ideas of who we are and how we should live. Mass resistance does not seem about to emerge. The logic of the market dominates in government, industry and mass media. Such debate as exists has more to do with details of whether and how much to regulate markets; there is near unanimity regarding the model of development it proposes and the conception of humans and of society on which it depends.

II

This essay contemplates the way in which the logic of the market disarticulates the relationships between cause and effect and how this, in turn, facilitates the normalisation, even justification, of *adharma* whether in the socioeconomic sphere or in the realm of individual conduct. I understand adharma to be the consequence of acting on a basis that negates our mutuality, equality and shared destiny with all that exists on this planet. Much of what is valorised today requires us, in one way or other, to ignore such considerations. This obscures the violence of what the ascendant norm proposes as rational and necessary for individual freedom as well as socioeconomic development.

Within the logic of the market, the relationship between actions and their consequences is treated in a number of ways. One strategy is to dispute that such a relationship exists; for example, denial of the impact on children of violent video games or of futures trading on the price of commodities. Another is to contest any proof that may be offered; this seems the preferred mode of dealing with the impact of climate change or of air, water and industrial pollution on health. A third is to deem the consequence a small price to pay. It is in this way that critique of the devastating human, social and ecological costs of neoliberal development is routinely dismissed.

It is at times also proposed that the consequence of an action is not a concern of any relevance to the actor. The implication is that individuals have the choice to refuse the offer being made. This is the typical response of advertisers and the mass media to any critique of them. On occasion a consequence is technically admitted but simultaneously disavowed as when the individual who suffers the outcome is blamed for it. This line of defence is often taken by companies who manufacture and sell substances like cigarettes or alcohol whose social desirability (which they assiduously promote) all but eclipses information regarding their addictive nature. Finally, there is the tactic of discrediting the persons or groups seeking to establish links between practices and their consequences whether with a view to their reform or prohibition. More than one of these approaches may be put to use in a given context.

What is striking about all six of these common strategies is that they are offensive in intent and defensive in nature. They are, in other words, attacks in defence of things as they are. None even pretends to address the ethical core of the challenges being posed to their way of seeing. The responses presume the historic necessity of development Euro-American style and privilege notions of freedom and choice either profitable to it or else congruent with it. Fundamental questions of ethics (whether a policy or practice is just) are evaded as the terrain of discussion shifts to the right of markets to operate freely and of consumers to buy as they please. The market emerges as a kind of secular God in which we should unwaveringly trust; its writ is considered final.

It is small wonder then that anti-capitalist dissidence is deemed suspect, irrational and heretical and often met with violence. Its spokespersons are pilloried and their arguments trivialised in trials by the media while those on the frontlines of this war — farmers, tribals, urban poor — are ruthlessly displaced. The brutality of this process barely seems to register in the consciousness of those who support neoliberal development. The ideological ground has already been prepared to enable this. Their faith in the model of economic development in whose interests the masses are being evicted is so complete, that the latter have been conceptually banished even prior to their physical dismissal. The end justifies and explicates the means.

A generalised culture of disregard for consequences assists in creating a sense of moral impunity. It is further facilitated by the celebrity status often conferred on those especially in power who 'get away with it'. Indeed, much of what counts for news these days is a serial reporting of politicians, sportspersons, film stars, corporate elites and other socialites in some kind of trouble (usually of their own making). News reports of these incidents turn on the issue of whether they will or will not get away with what they have done, who will come to their aid, what strategies they may use to extricate themselves and whether the incident will enhance or compromise their present standing. The rights and wrongs of the issue are rarely addressed. Indignation when it is expressed is often intermixed with a barely concealed admiration for the individual's hubris and the attention s/he has garnered. We have here what Williams called 'condoned fallibility'[3] with likeability as its shadow.[4]

The fascination for the trials and tribulations of individuals extends beyond celebrities to include unknown participants in reality television as also in music and other televised competitions. The panoply of human emotions unfolds before us in these shows: fear, hope, tension, sorrow, disappointment, envy, victory. The sense of identification between audience and contestant can be quite potent. Collective waves of relief and chagrin can be sensed from the responses of the studio audience and the text messages and emails of those watching from home. We cannot seem to get enough of these shows. What might be going on?

The intense interest in the stories of individuals, whether from elite or ordinary backgrounds, may lie in the fact that they offer a means by which to negotiate the sociocultural present. The impact of economic liberalisation has loosened the hold of the traditional family. Public discourse frequently trumps youth as India's demographic dividend. The greater economic independence has meant autonomy at a younger age. The commercial environment primarily addresses the young as individuals. The pressure to succeed, to act and look a certain way, to be part of a peer group, to adopt mores that may be unfamiliar or uncomfortable generates considerable tension and stress. Perhaps the contestants hold a mirror to the vulnerabilities, hopes, dilemmas, dreams, and nightmares of many, their frequently small-town origins providing the perfect analogue to the viewers' sense of feeling dwarfed by a demanding present and uncertain future.

These programmes are not, however, merely reflecting the sociocultural moment; they are actively shaping it. Their emergence is an aspect of public entertainment in the age of neoliberal transformation. The narrative of these shows turns on desire and its fulfilment or lack of fruition. The prizes are products whose allure is their desirability. Success brings adulation, even if only temporarily, though some individuals have gone on to careers in music, film and modelling. Personal appearance and presentation are important ingredients of success. These shows function to domesticate the market and its assumptions. They contribute to the idea that our desire to look good, succeed and be popular is natural, not socially constructed. They play a role in securing our acceptance of an economy that urges us to fulfil our aspirations through its products and services. It would appear that to refuse would be to suppress our very natures.

III

Social formations are characterised by multiplicity not
homogeneity. The neoliberal logic though dominant in certain
sectors coexists with others. Feudal social relations predominate
in much of India. Here consumerism has been embraced
but the permissive social mores of neoliberalism have been
challenged. Violence and 'moral' policing have followed. Youth
and young adults have borne the burden of navigating the
uneasy relationships and points of conflict between frameworks.

The feudal order did not need to obscure its hierarchies or
dissimulate their effects. It has been confident of gender, caste
and age as self-evident prerogatives. Its rhetoric is explicit and
unapologetic. Its violence though contested has been socially
acceptable. Its adharma, its negation of equality, mutuality
and shared destiny, has been plain for us to see.

Neoliberalism represents a different kind of sociocultural
order. It does not privilege ascribed identities. It arrives
on Indian shores with the economic and political might
of the West behind it. Science, technology and reason are
emblazoned on its shield. 'Freedom' and 'choice' are central
to its verbal arsenal. Profit is its bottom line. Its commitment
to democracy is thus provisional; its support is contingent on
whether the market will be permitted to function unfettered.
It has had to work within certain constraints given India's
political history though the nation's laws and regulatory
structures have been gradually dismantled for its benefit. Its
adharma is both evident and not so evident.

We have a well-developed and astute critique of the economic,
political and ecological impact of neoliberal development.

But we have paid scant attention to its sociocultural consequences. Two reasons may be proposed for this. First, most critics of development also subscribe to this paradigm; their objections primarily lie in the failure of the state to control market forces to ensure that development proceeds in a phased and equitable manner that benefits all. Second, many of us welcome the weakening of a patriarchal feudal order that these changes have facilitated. It is genuinely possible for many today to contemplate life trajectories that would previously have been unthinkable. In affirming these positive changes we too have used the language of choice and freedom.

We have, however, fallen short in our failure to notice the challenges that have emerged alongside these new possibilities. Neoliberalism is not merely a political force to be confronted. It also poses existential questions to be explored. We are not as capital would wish: desire-driven consumers who freely choose to commit ourselves to its regime since it can best meet our supposedly innate and ever increasing need for more of everything. These premises frame much of what is considered fun, exciting or entertaining today. We have neither countered these assumptions nor its cynical view of human nature.

Critique is never merely negative; it comprises equally of an alternative vision of how things could be. If our politics are to offer a way forward we will have to directly confront the disregard of consequences at the heart of the neoliberal discourse of freedom and choice. This rhetoric has served to mask its violence in the social and personal arenas even as it has secured our subjection to the logic of the market. We will in other words have to engage with the ethical. Else we too will be evading the issue of consequences.

Notes

1. Raymond Williams, 'Humanity', in *Keywords: A Vocabulary of Culture and Society*, London: Fontana/Croon Helm, 1976, pp. 123–24.
2. Ibid.
3. Ibid., p. 123.
4. This essay was written before Anna Hazare's anti-corruption campaign that briefly caught the national imagination between April and August 2011. But to the degree that the campaign advanced a simplistic analysis of corruption and proposed a deeply undemocratic solution, it failed to stimulate the kind of wide-ranging national introspection on ethics that is sorely overdue. Media coverage which did much to make the issue 'national' proceeded along predictable lines viewing politics as a contest over power not a debate over principles with the focus (especially on television) on who was going to win rather than what was going to be won. With Anna Hazare and his own team also frequently speaking in these terms, the possibility for serious, sustained inquiry was never realised.

It Leaves You Wanting More

It would not be an exaggeration to consider desire to be the engine of the skewed model of development that we are currently pursuing. Neoliberalism has sanctified the profit motive and projected even corporate greed as a virtue from which we all stand to benefit. The 'growth' economy has been characterised by a proliferation of desires and the sale of goods and services intended to meet them. The process has blurred, even welded together, the lines between needs, hopes, longings and aspirations in those who can afford these products. But there seems to be a catch. It turns out that these desires can be ambiguous, at times hard to grasp and not always easy to satiate. The ensuing sense of something still to be experienced is suggestive of the Latin root of desire which combines the sense of want with regret.

One illustration of this convergence are positive testimonials (whether of travel, books or gadgets) that often end with the wistful implication, if not explicit statement that, 'it leaves you wanting more'. The declaration is not intended to point to something lacking. To the contrary, it is a compliment. The person intends to convey that the experience was so good that it goes without saying that one would want more. This curious presumption invites our attention.

If something truly satisfies, one's experience of it should leave one contented. If one is left wanting more, then either the experience fails to meet its promise in some way, or else one's expectations of it have been unreasonable, or there is something about the nature of the experience that generates the desire for ever more. However, the testifier in our example intends none of these interpretations. So let us return to them having first examined what underlies the statement as it is meant to be understood.

The expression 'it leaves you wanting more' is founded in an assumption, currently widely shared, that one can never have enough of a good thing. This depends on two interlinked ideas: that desire is naturally occurring and that it is by its very nature impossible to fully satisfy. The logic is circular. Desire is natural and will always exist. And since it is natural and will always exist, it will be impossible for it to be completely fulfilled. There will always be something more or something else that one will desire next.

Hinduism, Buddhism and neoliberalism would concur with this understanding of desire. The two religions identify desire as a site of suffering. Their methods for addressing it range from crude instructions to simply transcend it, to nuanced teachings which invite us to comprehend the root of desire, its transitory nature and the fleeting satisfaction it often yields. For neoliberalism desire is not a problem to be resolved but a fact to be celebrated; it is the motor force and very rationale of commerce. This focus on the nature of desire has left unexplored questions about the nature of the experiences through which yearnings are sought to be met. As we will see, this too has a bearing on the issue of satisfaction.

II

If there is one wish that manifestly unites our society in the present it would arguably be the desire to communicate. We seem to be a nation on the gab. Whether it is cell phones, text messages, emails or talk radio, it seems we cannot say enough, say it fast enough, find enough people to listen to us or sufficient means with which express ourselves. The technology we employ reflects what we can access: PCO (public call office) booths and cell phones at one end and in addition, emails, social media, text messaging, chatrooms, blogs, and Twitter at the other. The function of communication seems to have undergone a dramatic transformation. It has acquired a performative dimension.

Communication is no longer merely utilitarian. The telephone is not the talking-telegram of yesteryear, an instrument used sparingly to convey information of consequence. Much of what we say is frequently of little use to others. What seems to matter is the fact that we are communicating. We want to be read, heard and seen. And we are willing to share minute details of our day, every shade of thought, feeling or experience whether or not the people who are reading or listening to us are known to us or we to them. It is the act of communication that seemingly matters. I communicate therefore I am.

It is in this context that we may locate the emergence and frequent use of the word 'connectivity'. The term has the advantage of simultaneously referring to several modes of bridging time and space, from transportation to oral and written communication. A veritable explosion of new terms has been evident as each technology has made its own contribution to our lexicon: email, short message service (SMS), text message, blog, tweet. Why has connectivity come to be the preferred overarching word for what these changes cumulatively make possible? Is there perhaps a clue to be found here in our quest to understand the dance of desire and dissatisfaction?

'Connectivity' may be broken up into 'connective' and 'ity'. 'Connective' refers to the linking, the sharing and the means that make both possible. The suffix 'ity' denotes character, condition or state. 'Connectivity' signals the state, character or condition of being connected. In many ways it seems an accurate description of what prevails today. Far more people than ever before are in a continual state of being connected employing various technologies to this end. However, the word emphasises a condition of being over that which is being shared; put another way, it draws attention to the state of being connected more than the nature and character of the connection and communication. And it is in this gap, in the difference between the two, that desire and discontent may be seen to be chasing each other in circles.

It has become quite common to see individuals who have set off on a group outing each talking on their cell phones. One has also been part of gatherings at which many present send and receive a continual stream of text messages. Some of these exchanges may be important, even urgent. But it is unlikely that the bulk of them fall into this category. There are simply too many people engaged in such practices for this to be the case. It is more that many have become habituated to being wired to their favourite communication device, to demonstrating that the location at which they are physically present is only one of the many to which they are connected. Being kept apart from one's multitudinous affiliations even for a short spell of time appears to have become challenging and undesirable. It is as if wherever one may be it is one's relationships to those who are elsewhere that really matter, or at the very least that these other connections matter just as much.

This phenomenon illustrates the way the virtual has come to mediate our lives. The promise of the virtual is that it can render immaterial the constraints of time, space and physicality. The examples are many and well known. Technology can put us in instantaneous touch with people in other places, vast amounts of data can travel swiftly to facilitate collaborations among people scattered in several parts of the globe, jobs can be off-shored, work outsourced. We can take virtual tours of museums in other countries without leaving our desks. X-rays and medical reports can be uploaded and despatched for a second opinion with the click of a mouse. Civic-minded citizens and social justice activists can form virtual communities with specific objectives, share expertise and propose concrete resolutions to existing problems. These technologies have also been a boon to the elderly, the ill and the home-bound. At its best, for those who can afford them, the communications and technological revolutions have democratised access to information and facilitated new forms of affiliation and solidarity.

There are, however, limits to how far the virtual can subordinate the visceral. The diminishing returns of pretending that physicality can be rendered elastic and/or contingent are already evident. The relentless pace of work has led to serious health problems among employees in the technology sector requiring fresh batches of recruits to take up the grind. The nature of these problems directly challenges the premise that time and space can be compressed at will and without consequences. The young who predominate in technology are facing medical problems directly related to workplace routines (disrupted biorhythms, repetitive motion disorders) and other problems previously associated with an older age group (blood pressure, hypertension, diabetes, heart disease). These are some of the better-documented visceral and real-time effects of an intimate relationship with virtual technologies in a neoliberal context.[1]

There are other consequences whose implications have educationists and employers concerned: a noticeable decrease in the ability to concentrate on an issue or task over an prolonged period among heavy users of computers, video games and other devices. Here we move well beyond the high-tech industry. Our attention span seems to have shrunk; to be tied to the prospect of quick results or resolutions. It seems as if the volume and velocity of the information and stimuli to which we are simultaneously and continually exposed has affected our ability to retain focus and interest. A tendency towards distraction seems to be the result. The traces of this are everywhere to be seen, from the preference for bite-sized communication to the quest for continual stimulation. Text messages, blogs and Twitter satisfy both, which perhaps accounts for their popularity.

There is a direct relationship between our ability to focus and our ability to enjoy. Contrary to media and market wisdom (the two being almost indistinguishable in our time) enjoyment is not a consequence of the things we do but an effect of the degree to which we are fully present while doing them. Enjoyment fundamentally lies in the process. To experience it we need to be present not just physically but also mentally and emotionally. A tendency towards distraction detracts from this possibility. If our attention is constantly split between our handheld device and what is happening around us chances are that we cannot be adequately present to either. The result is a residual sense of incompleteness, of something that does not entirely satisfy.

Much has been made of the capacity to multitask. It is important to recognise the context for this, namely, the neoliberal drive to minimise costs while optimising labour, markets and profits. But the demand that we do many things at once requires forfeiting the kind of awareness that sustains pleasure. Without real focus it is as if our attention is surfing without pausing long enough on anything whether to take its measure or to give and receive from it. We end up skimming the many surfaces of life. Such an argument is an anathema to a politics that celebrates fragmentation, depthlessness and the ludic possibilities of the digital age. I have no quarrel with those who find sufficiency in its pleasures. My observations address the many signs that digital dependence has an addictive dimension.

An 'addiction' is a habitual inclination; a restless and repetitive attempt to satiate a felt hunger whose real root one may or may not be conscious of. But the substances or activities to which one is addicted frequently fail to deliver anything more than a temporary lifting of the spirits. Despite this the habit can be hard to break and can fully absorb the time and focus of one so dependent. The word is generally reserved for habitual inclinations that are injurious to one's physical and mental wellbeing.

What is it that people are seeking through these various devices which enable rapid forms of communication? Why is it that they fail to satisfy? And what facilitates an addictive relationship to them? The answers are no doubt complex and require research. But one can offer initial speculations. We are witness to an irony. The desire to reach out and to be heard is at the heart of this phenomenon of continual communication. It is this wish that the devices promise to fulfil in faster and ever new ways. But the very speed, accessibility and technology serve to undermine the quality and character of our interactions. One could say that we have been enabled to do more but at the price of experiencing a kind of connectivity which is perhaps other than what we may be seeking.

The word 'attention' comes from the Latin *attendere* which means 'to stretch toward' or 'give heed to'. It conjures the way we may physically lean toward someone to whom we are closely listening. To give heed is to mind, to regard with care, to take careful note of, to consider. Care, concern and reciprocity are evoked as also a measured temporality. 'Attention' is closely allied to communication in the sense of communing. The manner in which we generally use our devices (to declare, announce and inform, often instantaneously) suggests something entirely different. If one were to borrow an image from another age, we are rather more like the town crier than the family physician who listens closely or speaks consideredly. It is perhaps not coincidental that it is the word 'accessible' that is heard most frequently not other terms related to the communicative process. It expresses the condition or state of being available, not the quality of what is accessible or on offer.

The communications frenzy we witness today suggests that something about the way we speak and listen to each other does not entirely satisfy. This discontent is a consequence of the dispersal of our attention. 'Distraction' comes from the Latin *distractus*, which means to draw apart or pull in different directions. It is, as we know, the opposite of attention. Its synonyms include 'perplexity', 'disturbance', 'disorder', 'diversion' and 'frenzy'. This is the price of multitasking, our own as well as that of our digital devices. The very innovations that facilitate contact have created the conditions that scatter our focus and pull us apart. The technology initiates a dynamic that is simultaneously centrifugal and centripetal. It is the ideal context for an addictive relationship; it can never fully deliver but there is just enough to keep us searching, hoping and wishing for more.

Technology is not merely a tool. It reorganises perception and generates its own longings. We need neither fear it nor unambiguously celebrate it. However, we must analyse the way we have come to use it and be used by it; how social practices have been remade in this process. Examining the (inter)relations of the virtual and the visceral in all their lived complexity is crucial to such an inquiry. It is a question to which we will return.

Note

1. It is not my argument that the rise in health problems such as hypertension, diabetes or heart disease is attributable solely to technology or the culture of work. Other factors such as dietary shifts are equally

responsible. But these are also related to the complex of changes that have characterised the post-liberalisation period. The exponential growth of the market for fast foods, colas, desserts and snacks rich in fat and sugar is directly related to the greater disposable income, longer work hours and the increased desirability of dining out that have accompanied this transition.

INTIMACY

My understanding of intimacy has undergone a gradual
transformation. Previously, the word primarily referred
(as it commonly still does) to the relationship between an
individual and her or his partner, though in its sense as
emotional closeness, intimacy extended to close friends and
family members as well. As meditation helped me discover
my interconnectedness with a range of entities and energies,
the term slowly transmuted to indicate the experience
of being present. I came to realise that the sensuous and
nourishing experience of being fully attentive and having the
gift of the same from another had been constricted, making
for a reductive conception of intimacy. As a consequence
I had become estranged from the countless intimacies of
everyday life.

Intimacy is about the quality of an interaction, the nature
of our awareness, the intent with which we approach what
is before us. It is premised on an openness and friendliness
toward life. We experience it whenever we are present to

each other, even if only for a split second. Whether it is a meeting of the eyes, a hug, an act of kindness, a moment of shared acknowledgement with a stranger or friend, if we are fully present we experience intimacy. It is not, however, a practice that is outward in orientation. One cannot be present to others unless one is also present to oneself. It is this simultaneity of awareness that makes possible the richness of the connection that we describe as intimacy.

As we practice meeting life in this way, we learn that we can experience intimacy not merely with humans and animals but also with nature: sky, tree, landscape, cloud, bird, moth, river, ocean. To receive the rest of nature in this way we simply need to open to its aliveness; not merely to its dynamic propensities but to its capacity to manifest and communicate something of its beingness. As we do this, we learn that nature is not passive but actively reaching out to us. The rest of nature is always present in its fullness, just as it is. It is this characteristic that relaxes and restores us even when we are preoccupied. The same may be said of the human experience of receiving unconditional love from animals. We are soothed by their warmth and affection even when we are inattentive. Our joy multiplies exponentially when we reciprocate.

It is presentness — temporal, emotional and mental — that energises us and imbues us with the sense of fulfilment that we associate with intimacy. Yet we rarely extend it to ourselves and to each other, leading to the general dissatisfaction with interpersonal relationships so often expressed. If we could only recognise being present as the source of the pleasure of intimacy we could deepen and broaden our experience of it. Our sense of kinship would naturally widen to include affinities and forms of relating that are currently excluded. We would be free to experience our true intimacy with all that is.

ROOT VIBRATION

I still recall the first time it occurred to me to wonder whether the universe had a root vibration. I had put on some music and was sitting on a stone bench in the veranda. The apartment I was living in was on the third floor of a building that overlooked a vast open space.

Kites were gliding amiably in the morning sky, two of them playing the game of weaving close then veering off just as their wings were about to touch. They seemed to be having fun. The tall bamboo leaned into the breeze, its elongated leaves quivering gently. Dragonflies whirred busily while the occasional butterfly flitted below.

As I watched I began to realise something intriguing. The bamboo, the birds, the insects and the music seemed to be related in some integral way. It was not that the kites, the bamboo, the dragonflies and the butterflies were moving to the rhythm of the music. The pace of each was distinct. The kites were hanging, dipping and rising as they pleased. The bamboo, for its part, had surrendered to the breeze. No two leaves were identical in their tremulous motion. The dragonflies rose and fell in a gentle wave-like pattern while the butterflies moved swiftly. The relationship I sensed was not about tempo. Nor was it about the fact that all were in the same time-space. It was, rather, as if they were somehow congruent. But with what?

I resisted the temptation to make sense of what was happening. I softened my gaze and kept sitting. Three bee-eaters alighted briefly on the telegraph wire in the foreground. Within seconds they leapt off, flew in small circles their wings fanned out and then returned to their perch. They too seemed to be part of the harmony. As were the red-vented bulbuls with their jerky, helicopter-like movements.

Just then two men appeared and started walking casually along the mud road. Somehow their presence was not consonant with everything else. I cannot say they disturbed the scene in any way. But they diverged from the rest. Another man followed wheeling his bicycle beside him. He, on the other hand, seemed to belong. Three dogs ran alongside him. Two of them were, like the cyclist, in accord with whatever it was. The third was not.

What was it that connected so much of what was before me? And why were there some elements that did not seem to fit? I could not linger on the patio that day but I have had similar experiences since then. Each time I am led to the same questions.

It has become clear over time that the concordance between things is not related to the genre of music. Jimi Hendrix, Jim Morrison, J. S. Bach, G. F. Handel, Sanjay Subrahmanyan, flamenco, avant-garde jazz, Rajasthani folk music: all have yielded this same sense of congruence. And nature does not have to be doing anything in particular for it to be possible. The trees may look listless in the heat, be sighing in the breeze or be lashed by monsoon winds. The grass may be lush or the landscape dry as a bone. Birds may be plentiful or absent, insects in plain view or not. But certain musicians and certain pieces of music seem to manifest a vibration that corresponds with insects, birds and plant life. And some humans and animals seem to evince the same.

Is there a root vibration? Does nature always express it? Why are only some humans in tune with it and not others? What facilitates alignment with this vibration, and by the same token, what detracts? Does the fact that dogs are only sometimes at one with it have anything to do with their proximity to humans?

There are other puzzles. What is it that enables brilliant but personally troubled musicians to express unison with it? Is it the purity of their intent? The intensity of their focus? The force of their imagination? Perhaps all three as they combine to propitiate and provoke the spirit of music into healing them and through them their listeners?

Many questions. No answers. I share them in the hope that others may conduct their own experiments and help resolve the mysteries hinted at in these moments of harmonic convergence.

MAVERICK DESIGNS: ON DIESEL JEANS AND GEOENGINEERING

In 2010, Diesel launched a campaign headlined, 'Be Stupid'. The series won a Grand Prix in the outdoor category that year at the Cannes Lions International Festival of Creativity, a prestigious industry award. The March issue of the Indian edition of *GQ*, an upscale men's magazine, carried a four-page fold-out advertisement.

On one page a young man in blue jeans is astride the trunk of an elephant. He holds the tip of the tusker's trunk between his hands and looks over his shoulder at an indeterminate spot. The elephant is looking at the ground. The second is a two-page spread of a young bikini-clad woman standing in a grassy meadow. She is intently gazing into her underwear and taking a photograph of what she sees there. A lion is closing in on her from the rear. But she seems oblivious of this fact. Yellow block letters printed partially over lion, tree and grass declare, 'Smart may have the brains, but stupid has the balls'. Beneath, in smaller type, are the words, 'Be Stupid' and beside it the logo, 'Diesel: For Successful Living'. The fourth page repeats

'Be Stupid', in bold blue letters on a jet black page and in the bottom right corner is the brand's logo.

Diesel's primary product is denim although it also designs and markets other fashion items including sunglasses, bags, shoes, underwear. When asked about the idea behind the campaign, Renzo Rosso, the founder of the company, had this to say: 'The campaign is about how stupid I have felt over the last 30 years. I've tried many new things and sometimes I have felt really stupid because people didn't understand. Now with the global crisis, consumers want something new. Stupid people see how things could be, not how things are. They look to the future, shape a vision and are braver'.[1] It would be easy enough to dismiss the campaign as just another instance of the kind of transgressive representation currently in vogue. But the nature of its provocation and Rosso's explanation compel us to pause and reflect.

II

We live in an interesting time. On the one hand we receive multiple daily reminders that doomsday may be upon us given the way we carelessly continue to overexploit nature's resources. On the other hand the very forces responsible for this devastation are avidly celebrated. For the most part we tend to think of the warnings and the glorification as discrete phenomena. The advertisement for Diesel illustrates that it is not quite so simple. It stages a drama that explicitly incorporates several contemporary flashpoints though it does so in its own particular way.

The advertisement plays with a number of themes that characterise the present: the altered relationship of humans and wild animals as development and tourism encroach upon forest land; the pleasure and danger of changing sexual mores as they conflict with existing conventions; a subculture of narcissism that is the combined effect of the heightened concern with physical appearance and the valorising of individualism; the tendency to document and share every experience, a desire enabled and fuelled by new technologies; a scrambling of the borders between public and private; and specific to India, the greater public visibility in the last decade of middle- and upper-class urban women as sexually self-determining.

The backdrop and explicit points of reference for the Indian reception of this advertisement are the economic and social transformations that have accompanied neoliberal globalisation. But the new order is unstable, still a work in progress. Many relationships are askew and, to borrow a phrase coined by Mary Douglas in another context, there is a great deal of 'matter out of place'.[2] It is in this context that the advertisement circulates and the strange physical proximity of the models to the animals gathers an additional, local valence. In one image the man stands with an elephant trunk between his legs and in another the woman is so absorbed in taking a photo of her pubic hair (for what else could her camera capture at the angle at which it is being held?) that she does not even sense the lion at her rear. The direction of the young man's gaze also implies the presence of a camera. Despite holding its trunk between his legs he looks not at the elephant but off to the side. He seems more conscious of the photo opportunity than of his experience in the moment.

The oddness of this proximity is also manifest in the animals. The elephant looks unnaturally aloof despite its trunk being

in the hands of an unknown human. It gives the impression
of being a cardboard cut-out with which one might pose in
a fairground. The expression on the lion's face is likewise
discordant. The composition was most likely enabled by
Photoshop, a software program that allows one to cut, paste
and merge images. For instance, the model can be shot in
a photo studio and then placed in a photograph of a grassy
meadow (given what she is doing this might be a good
thing). The image of the lion can be imported and the copy
superimposed. Photoshop lends a whole new dimension to the
notion of simulacrum.

Renzo Rosso and his brand managers are likely to consider the
advertisement's lack of realism as beside the point. Campaigns
frequently strive to evoke ideas with which they would like
their brand to be associated. This goal can at times take
precedence over representation of the product. The Diesel
advertisement conjures particular notions of adventure,
unconventionalism, risk-taking, sexual self-expression,
individuality. The young man and woman are shown doing
the unexpected, doing so publicly and having themselves
photographed in the process.

III

The disjunction between the advertisement and 'reality' may
be inconsequential to the advertiser. But it is crucial to an
understanding of the cultural logic of neoliberal modernity.
Within its discourse, innovation, courage and visionary
thinking lie precisely in not permitting ground realities to
limit, deflect or constrain one's imagination and aspirations.
Neoliberalism's heroes are most often those who are said to

have defied prevailing conditions and conventional wisdom to carve their own, supposedly individual, route to prosperity. Success would seem predicated on either ignoring what exists or else in transforming it; never in making concessions or adjusting to it.

A predisposition toward disregarding consequences naturally follows as also the tendency to consider boundaries and borders as there to be breached in the pursuit of success. Neoliberalism's idea of achievement is effectively independent of any reckoning of its impact whether in the personal, social, political or environmental arenas. Success is deemed its own rationale. The 'Official Be Stupid Philosophy' video posted on YouTube states the matter succinctly: 'Stupid is the relentless pursuit of a regret free life'.[3]

It is in this setting that the print advertisement for Diesel begins to make some kind of sense. We see adult humans in an unusual relationship with animals, courting sure danger in one case and potentially in the other also. Both individuals are self-absorbed, each in their own way. The elephant is akin to a prop and the meadow a stage-set for the female model's experiment with photographing herself. Both what they are shown to be doing and where they are shown to be doing it suggests they have little to no understanding of their location and how to relate appropriately to it. One could consider them foolish. The copy is ruder. It dubs them 'stupid'. But it does so approvingly. 'Smart may have the brains, but stupid has the balls'. It aligns 'stupid' with 'courage' and 'daring' and although it codes both as masculine ('has the balls') it is a woman who is shown to express these qualities in the most startling manner, attesting to the greater fluidity of gender in the present.

Rosso's interview is also pertinent here although most people who see the advertisement are unlikely to have read it. In his mind the campaign is related to his having felt stupid over the years because people did not understand him. But given his resounding success the implication is that his having felt this way was not a result of a lack of intelligence on his part, but an absence of its appreciation by others. He exhorts us to be like him: brave enough to be stupid in crafting a daring vision for the future.

The advertisement for Diesel expresses an idea at the core of neoliberal discourse: that the rest of nature exists to enable humans to realise its notion of 'successful living'. Nature is seen as a resource or backdrop but not as a living entity that can and does act to limit human action and possibility. Neoliberalism adopts a similar perspective on socioeconomic and cultural realities.

This disregard of what prevails is evident in its conception of innovation. True innovators are those who are seen to break with established convention; to remake what exists in order to realise a desire, dream, idea or goal. It is true that the act of making or creating inevitably involves the rearrangement of matter. We may also agree that many things are indeed in need of being transformed. However, when such action is undertaken from a premise that the matter that is rearticulated has no integrity of its own, that there is no need to take account of the interrelationships of nature or for that matter of prevailing culture, then we are predisposed to privileging innovation per se; to imagining that it can be divorced from the question of its implications and consequences. We create the conditions in which geoengineering can be deemed a credible way of coping with the challenge of climate change. I hope the reader will bear with me as I make my case and also argue its relationship to my analysis of the Diesel campaign.

IV

Geoengineering is an intentional intervention in the Earth's oceans, soil and atmosphere aimed at containing the impact of climate change.[4] It is the search for a quick-fix solution to the cumulative consequences of unbridled industrialisation. Unlike adaptation strategies that call for a fundamental revisioning of how we live, it would not require the industrialised countries or the wealthy in developing economies to give up the lifestyle they have come to regard as their due. As Richard Branson, owner of Virgin Airlines and keen investor in geoengineering projects put it, 'If we could come up with a geoengineering answer to this problem, then Copenhagen wouldn't be necessary. We could carry on flying our planes and driving our cars'.[5]

A number of audacious proposals have emerged. These include 'fertilising' the ocean with iron nanoparticles to increase phytoplankton that would theoretically sequester carbon dioxide; burning biomass through pyrolysis in low-oxygen environments and burying the concentrated carbon in the soil; building 16 trillion space sun shades to deflect sunlight 1.5 million kilometres from the earth; launching thousands of ships with turbines to propel salt spray to whiten clouds and thereby deflect sunlight; changing the acidity of the ocean with limestone so that it can soak up extra carbon dioxide; blasting sulphate-based aerosols into the stratosphere to defect sunlight; covering deserts with white plastic to reflect sunlight; putting a superfine reflective mesh of aluminium threads between the Earth and the sun; cloud seeding to precipitate rainfall; and technologies to prevent storm formation.

None of these proposals actually treat the root of the problem, namely, the need to reduce greenhouse gas emissions. They are all strategies of containment intended to retain the current status quo. Some aim at countering the effects of greenhouse gases by blocking incoming sunlight or by redirecting the radiation of sunlight back into space (space shades, covering deserts with plastic material, for example). Others attempt to remove and sequester the carbon dioxide after its release into the atmosphere (for instance, through biochar technologies or ocean fertilisation methods seeking to increase carbon dioxide absorption via altering the sea's chemical balance). A third approach is to intervene in the weather pattern itself, to generate rainfall or restrain storms from forming by dropping chemicals into clouds, burning forests, and so on.

The science of these proposals is theoretical at best. The technologies are proposed on the basis of assumptions that are debatable. For instance, it is not proven that it is iron deficiency that accounts for diminishing phytoplankton in the world's oceans. The promised outcome of this strategy is also uncertain. If we keep with the ocean fertilisation example, adding iron nanoparticles may increase algae blooms but there is no guarantee that it would result in an increased capture and elimination of carbon. Most importantly, the proposals fail to address the wider consequences of such interventions. In the example at hand these include the potential for oxygen depletion in the deep sea, disruption of marine ecosystems, increased releases of other greenhouse gases, the worsening of ocean acidification and the disruption of the livelihoods of fishing communities.[6]

The hubris of these proposals is striking. They presume that one can mimic, cheat and short circuit nature through technological intervention and do so without initiating a chain of unintended effects whose impact may be far worse than what currently confronts us. Not only are the consequences of proposed interventions not squarely addressed, scant attention has been paid to the effects of suspending them once they have been carried out. Even to a non-scientist, the idea that one can selectively tamper with processes that are inherently and intricately interlinked seems patently absurd. That there is a renewed interest in these proposals in recent years on the part of industry, science and government in Canada, the United States (US) and the UK is indicative of their desperation to do nothing to imperil business as usual. Even a crisis as grave as the one we collectively face seems unable to dislodge a perspective that pretends that humanity can treat nature as it pleases and even beat it at its own game.

The shared conceptual underpinnings of geoengineering and the 'Be Stupid' campaign are hopefully obvious enough by this point to not need belabouring. They lie at two ends of a single spectrum. It may be tempting to see one as about fashion and therefore trivial and the other as about science and accordingly serious. But that would be a mistake. The Diesel advertisement plays a part (amplified by other advertisers who adopt a like perspective) in creating the conditions that make the fantasies of geoengineering seem plausible. It encourages a culture of reckless risk-taking and disdain for reality and celebrates as mavericks those who transgress boundaries with no concern about the integrity of all that is violated in the process. This structurally aligns rule-breakers with the future and dismisses their critics as naysayers committed to the hidebound ways of the past. It is a short step from this to seeing geoengineers and their advocates as those who, as Renzo Rosso put it, 'see how things could be, not how things are ... [who] ... look to the future, shape a vision and are brave'.[7] But bravery combined with thoughtlessness is a deadly mix. Unless it is challenged, geoengineering may place humanity in a position analogous to the woman in the Diesel advertisement: vulnerable, defenceless and in the path of catastrophic danger.

Notes

1. Priyanka Khanna, 'It's in the Jeans', Interview with Renzo Rosso, *Vogue*, April 2010, p. 105.
2. Mary Douglas, *Purity and Danger: An Analysis of Concepts of Pollution and Taboo*, London: ARK Paperbacks, 1984, p. 35.
3. http://www.youtube.com/watch?v=Y4h8uOUConE (accessed 1 August 2012).
4. My discussion of geoengineering draws extensively on Diana Bronson, Pat Mooney and Kathy Jo Wetter, *Retooling the Planet: Climate Chaos in the Geoengineering Age*, Stockholm: Swedish Society for Nature Conservation, 2009.
5. Ibid., p. 14.
6. Ibid., pp. 19–28.
7. Khanna, 'It's in the Jeans', p. 105.

BEYOND ANTITHESIS

Theory and politics in the past several decades have combined
to challenge unitary wholes as social constructions that
are hierarchical in structure, intolerant of difference and
discriminatory in intent and practice. 'Race', 'nation', 'gender',
'family', and 'sexuality' are potent examples of ideas in relation
to which this argument has been thoroughly and convincingly
elaborated. The content of each has been successfully
pluralised. It is no longer possible to speak fluently of them in
singular terms despite continued efforts to do just that.

The process has not been unidirectional. The self-conscious
crafting and claiming of individual identity and sexuality, even
family or community, from a multiplicity of factors — some
chosen, some ascribed — has not precluded seeing others
in essentialist terms. For example, individuals and groups
that have argued for such a rethinking have also supported
a unitary conception of nation with a xenophobic prejudice
against particular communities. As a result, even as some
have celebrated the emergence of new cultural expressions
others have needed to insist on the integrity of existing ones.

Public discourse today is thus marked by a mix of old and new conceptions.

This essay reflects on some of the consequences of the critique of holism and makes a case for its reconsideration. The original challenge to the positing of unitary wholes stemmed from a radical impulse. Such constructs, it was correctly argued, generalised particular forms as normative, proscribed others as deviant; or else derided them as wanting in some way. For example, so long as only the heterosexual family was regarded as normative other kinds of relationships, shared commitments and household units could not receive the social and legal recognition that they equally deserved. Likewise, if the unstated though presumed ideal citizen was Hindu or white the experience vis-à-vis state institutions of those from other religious or racial groups was likely to be shaped by this prejudice.

To the degree that normative categories imply judgements they evoke not merely hierarchy but also morality. Religion, custom, even science, was thus marshalled in support of the dominant norm. All three were most often conceived as unchanging, non-conflictual, naturally occurring, unitary wholes. In this context critique proceeded by illustrating the historical basis of what has come to be considered the norm and thus the social and political character of claims about their 'naturalness'. Documenting diversity, conflict and change over time became crucial to challenging a given norm.

It was in this context that hybridity, heterogeneity, fragmentation, and discontinuity came to be affirmed. These concepts challenge the way normative categories smother and 'other' difference and deny history. The fictive nature of claims about purity was revealed by directing attention to the syncretism or mixing and melding that is integral to human life and sociocultural practice. A great deal of analytic energy was released as intellectual, social and artistic conventions were disputed. False universalisms were unmasked, and once their histories had been specified, were assigned a local place. Pluralising the content of concepts previously construed in homogeneous terms laid bare their relationship to structures of power. It also illustrated how the so-called marginal had in fact served to define the centre, whether explicitly or implicitly. Defiance of convention in the artistic realm took the shape of experiments with new subject matter and equally with form. Formal experimentation emerged as the resistant practice par excellence.

This intervention is variously described as post-structualist, postmodern and in some of its aspects as postcolonial. Poststructuralist notes a theoretical break, postcolonial a political rupture. 'Postmodern' is both a theoretical description and periodising term. The critique has recast academic disciplines as well as political and cultural imagination. Although it did not succeed in transforming the status quo, its vitality and impact have been significant. But like any movement it introduced its own protocols and preferences, exclusions and limitations. These shortcomings invite us to take another look at the effort so that we may move beyond the antithesis that this critique has, regrettably, come to represent.

II

Theoretical concepts are tools; like their mechanical counterparts they enable us to do particular things. But there ends the similarity. For where a carpenter is unlikely to use a screwdriver when the task calls for wrench, the analyst is vulnerable to concepts shaping her or his work: what it is able to notice, what it makes of what it identifies, and the relationships it posits between different aspects of what is being analysed. This vulnerability is not the fatal flaw of particular theories or concepts but the inevitable precondition of any cognitive effort. Physicists, philosophers and humanists now agree that objectivity is an article of faith; that the presence of the observer subtly alters that which is observed and that our knowledge is always situated. These insights do not require us to risk civilisational chaos by settling for relativism and unbridled subjectivism, the fears of those who cling to the notion of objectivity. The insight that knowledge is always partial and situated can lead instead to critical dispassion and humility.

It is the absence of these two qualities in the way that poststructuralist theory has by and large developed that has led to its having become an antithetical critique. Its insights have not always been applied to itself in a systematic way; consequently, it has not always been conscious of its own 'situatedness'. (As with any phenomenon there were exceptions.)[1] At the same time, poststructuralism's celebration of fragmentation, marginality, discontinuity, and non-narrative forms has made it indifferent to ideas, as also evidence, of wholeness, continuity, stability, and to linear narratives that express these dimensions of social experience. The a priori suspicion of holism has extended to the politics and poetics of such perspectives and representations. Or else the politics have been supported while silence maintained on the rhetoric and aesthetics of those living or documenting the struggles that speak in these terms. So it is that one can support 'the rights of displaced tribal communities' but without engaging the worldview in defence of which this struggle is undertaken. The net result has been that poststructuralism and postmodernism have been unable to take *theoretical* account of the continuing salience of that which they tend to disregard. Two ways of thinking, two kinds of work exist in parallel, separate and unequal, within a new hierarchy in which the poststructuralist and postmodern are the new norm.

It is important not to overstate the case. There is no necessary relationship between poststructuralist theory and a disinterest in linear narrative or holistic thinking. We are speaking here of how its practice has generally tended to evolve. Furthermore, poststructuralist concepts have been invaluable to indigenous movements in contesting, for example, the content of dubious or non-inclusive notions of authenticity and the basis on which such claims have been advanced. The problem rather has been the failure to simultaneously attend to wholeness as well as fragmentation, to continuity as well as discontinuity, to linear as well as non-narrative forms, and to do so with equal dispassion. To the extent that the theory consistently privileges the latter in each pair and remains wary of the former it cannot offer a new synthesis; a fresh way of thinking about their temporal simultaneity, their interrelationships where they exist and the non-homogeneous yet integral whole constituted by them. This shortcoming effectively consigns holistic thinking and linear narratives to a temporal past and positions poststructuralism as the avant-garde praxis that heralds the future.

Poststructuralism could have contributed to a new way of thinking about wholes: as internally differentiated integral structures that are the effect of the dynamics of continuity and discontinuity, diversity and commonality and the power relations that characterise a given historical moment. Instead it has enabled the proliferation of difference. And it has done so in ways that are frequently unconcerned with the similarities and resonances which could offer a basis for envisioning forms of solidarity and affiliation that are not contingent on sameness. In doing so it has both reflected and served to strengthen a broader socio-political trend: a politics of separation in which constituencies invested in their particularity and its presumed uniqueness compete for recognition, resources and representation in a republic of difference that is indifferent to commonality.

The move to pluralise concepts, identities and narratives should ideally be a kind of ground-clearing exercise that makes way for re-conceiving their relations to each other and to the whole of which they are a part. The problem is not holism per se but the way in which it has hitherto been constructed. To acknowledge holism is not to deny history. It is merely to state the obvious; that holistic ways of thinking persist across time and space and that we are all, in the end, part of a single, interconnected whole. These facts alone compel us to think through the intersections between concepts, narratives and identities. To fail to theorise their relatedness is to forfeit the promise of poststructuralism for a vacuous valorisation of difference that obscures our mutuality and deems as radical the mere transgression of social, political, sexual, and aesthetic norms and conventions.

Note

1. Donna Haraway, 'A Cyborg Manifesto: Science, Technology and Socialist Feminism in the Late Twentieth Century', in *Simians, Cyborgs and Women: The Reinvention of Nature*, New York: Routledge, 1991, pp. 145–81; Chela Sandoval, *Methodology of the Oppressed*, Minneapolis: University of Minnesota Press, 2000.

IN OTHER WORDS:
BEYOND ANTITHESIS, TAKE 2

We apprehend the world through the words we use and the ways in which we have come to understand them. Words can open our consciousness or narrow our perception, deepen sensation or deaden our capacity to feel. The struggle over language is intrinsic to politics. We invent new words to speak of things our vocabulary cannot quite express. Or we reclaim existing terms in ways that alter the meanings they have accrued.

Words are also windows. The root of words, their obsolete meanings, and the conventions regarding their use tell us something about their history and present. The changing uses and meanings of words register evolutions and transformations not just in language but in society's perceptual frames. In a small way, then, elements of the story of modernity may be traced through reflecting on the meanings of words.

II

I could have written these sentences in the 1980s when I was in graduate school. And they would have meant one thing.

But I write them now from a different place. To say a little about this requires a brief autobiographical detour. In 1993, I suffered a head injury because of unwittingly being in the path of a high-speed car chase in which the California highway patrol was in pursuit of a stolen vehicle. The ensuing collision threw me into a realm in which I could not count on elementary cognitive functions.

One surprising aspect of the difficult period that followed was the simultaneous experience of things that my theoretical outlook at the time of the accident would have posed as binary opposites: wholeness and fragmentation, essence and 'constructedness'. In ways that I cannot explain, I had a palpable sense of being whole even as my cumulative incapacities made both perception and daily life a discontinuous, fragmented experience. Alongside this, as fatigue and inability to concentrate made speech a challenge, I sensed what I can only describe as the essence of each person in my environment. It was with this that I communed most often without recourse to language. While this essence was not itself a product of history its hosts most certainly were. The idea of social construction continued to make sense. Alongside this growing awareness of the temporal simultaneity and equal validity of conceptions that I had assumed to be opposed, was gradual realisation of the interrelatedness of other aspects that I had believed to be quite distinct from each other. By way of example, a word.

III

'Inspiration': the word literally means 'in-breath'. Although the term is most often associated with a purely mental process, with the activity of consciousness, its constituent components ('in', 'spiration') speak to the indivisibility of the mental and the physical and to their connectedness with something larger than both. The breath enters the body from outside. Its movement through and beyond ensures our aliveness. We are because we breathe. Each in-breath and out-breath affirms the intimate relationship between mind, body and environment. All three are in dynamic interaction with one another. The nature of this relationship determines the texture and quality of life. Contemplated from this vantage point, 'environment' assumes its broadest dimensions, referring not merely to physical ecology but equally to the economic and sociocultural landscapes in which we exist. Our breath connects us with the entire phenomenal world.

IV

In stark contrast to the near constant activity that had previously characterised my days, I spent most of my time in silence, when possible gazing out of my bedroom window and sitting in the garden. Out in nature, even in an urban backyard, the sense of things as inextricably connected grew to resounding certainty. Could it be, I wondered, that our perception of interconnectedness had been somehow compromised? What could have led to its disaggregation, to our seeming incapacity to notice it?

V

'Integral' is derived from Late Latin, *integralis*, meaning 'untouched', 'whole', 'entire'. *Webster's* offers three senses of the term. Two are relevant here, the third being its mathematical definition. In its first sense, 'integral' is 'whole, entire, lacking nothing, complete as an entity'; in its second, 'making part of a whole, or necessary to make a whole'. The same word stands for the part as well as the whole of which it is a part. The parts are necessary to completing the whole, to its lacking nothing. Part and whole imply and require each other. Each is the sine qua non of the other.

'Integrity' is from the same root. It also has three senses but these are more similar than distinct. The first defines it as 'the quality or state of being complete; wholeness; entireness; unbroken state'. The second reiterates this as 'the entire, unimpaired state or quality of anything; perfect condition; soundness'. The third moves from characterising objects to persons, 'the quality or state of being of sound moral principle; uprightness, honesty and sincerity'.

If integral is a wholeness wherein the parts do not detract but are, rather, necessary to its completeness, integrity is the recognition and honouring of this principle. It is that state or quality that manifests the perfect condition, defined here as 'unbroken, unimpaired, sound'. Integrity is the effect of understanding the interrelations that comprise the whole. The absence of integrity or 'brokenness' is the result of not seeing the part as integral to the whole and thus not acting on that basis.

The moral dimension of integrity to be found here is extremely enabling. Integrity is a consequence of embracing relationality and holism as principles. It expresses an axiom. It cannot thus be deemed the exclusive property of particular kinds of persons. The words 'impairment' and 'brokenness' in the dictionary entry must be placed in this context. For they are being used not in a morally-loaded normative sense, but to name the consequences of violating wholeness conceived in integral terms. It is a spacious conception. It does not require one to exclude any part of the whole. It does not propose hierarchy as natural. At the same time, the shared root of 'integral' and 'integrity' places ethics at the very core of perception and action.

VI

In the instability of illness, words or phrases often arrived as though related in some way. But they just as quickly dissolved. Questions began to form inchoately and in fragments. Over time, as I grew better, they slowly cohered. Was the suspicion of wholes and the insistence on difference to the neglect of interconnectedness the consequence of collective misrecognition? Could it be that despite our understanding of the *social* construction of knowledge, we had somehow been so persuaded by certain power-laden expressions and claims to 'truth' that these had become near-exclusive points of reference? Had their miasma somehow made it difficult to observe what actually obtains in the material world where at some level everything implies, requires, and is in complex relation to everything else? Were we so haunted by the delusory projections of dominant ideologies that we effectively naturalised their constructions even as we claimed to be challenging them? How had we failed to distinguish between the material effects of power structures, which are all too real, and the unreality of their claims? And how could we definitively counter these claims if our own practice, in effect, reproduced some version of these falsehoods as we demanded our 'rights'?

VII

'If you are a poet, you will see clearly that there is a cloud
floating in this sheet of paper. Without a cloud there will be
no water; without water the trees cannot grow; and without
trees, you cannot make paper. So the cloud is in here' —
Zen Master, Thich Nhat Hahn.[1]

Self-Other-Majority-Minority-Urban-Rural-Rich-Poor-Male-
Female-Transgender . . . 'the cloud is in here'. Mind-body-
heart-psyche, 'the cloud is in here'.

VIII

Our language expresses this idea yet we do not notice.
Nature manifests it but we fail to see. We take as real
the disarticulation of the integral. So much so that even
everyday words do not serve to jolt us into reflecting on our
assumptions. A verb.

Remember. To mentally recollect. To bring to mind. But the
word conjoins body and mind. Re-member. From 're': 'again';
and 'member', from Latin, *membrum*: limb, part of the body,
any part, portion or division.

Remember, to put back together. Etymologically it is not
thoughts but limbs that are united. Memory is not merely of
the mind. Who remembers? Mind? Heart? Body? Psyche? Each
in ways distinct but finally inseparable.

IX

We seem unable to notice the worlds conjured by our words
suggesting that it is not language alone that constructs our

sense of reality. The material facts of globalisation are equally salient. The disaggregation of production and perception that began with the industrial revolution has been taken to a qualitatively different level. When consciousness is thus disarticulated and dispersed, cause–effect relations become harder to grasp. Consequences are rendered opaque. One reason perhaps why ethics as an issue barely registers in public discourse. Panic-stricken authoritarian morality is certainly evident, but not collective reflection on the basis of which actions might be meaningfully considered. Ecological movements are, for the most part, a refreshing exception to this rule. Testimony to the relationship of integrity to an integral view of things?

Heal, to make whole, from Anglo-Saxon, *hal*, whole. To bring together that which has been rent apart, dismembered.

And so it goes on. And on. The earth on its axis. We in its embrace.

Note

1. Thich Nhat Hanh, 'The Heart of Practice', in *Being Peace*, Berkeley, CA: Parallax Press, 1987.

FOR ALTHUSSER WITH LOVE

We are hailed by ideology, true
But also by indigo skies
lilac jacarandas
the perfectly held note
the wrinkled beauty of age

If only we allowed ourselves
to be interpellated by these!
Perhaps we would be less captive to power
more open to the worlds
they summon for us

RECONJUGATING
LAW AND DHARMA

Notions of the sacred are central to societies in South Asia, whether as cultural sub-stratum, source of personal conviction or the bedrock of institutionalised religion. Yet, for the most part, as advocates of social change we have preferred to express our vision of equality and justice in predominantly secular terms drawing either on liberal-democratic or Left traditions. The violence of religion, both past and present, has all but eclipsed its equally potent legacy as a source of knowledge and inspiration for questions that lie at the heart of social justice activism: how to take one's place in the universe and within the human collectivity, what it means to be human. Our ensuing lack of fluency in the faith traditions of the subcontinent has made us ill-equipped to integrate into our search for justice, ethical conceptions derived from the emancipatory seam within this rich civilisational inheritance.[1]

The crises that continue to convulse our region compel us to develop toward the sacred or religious the kind of critical dispassion that we routinely evince in relation to liberalism or Marxism whose histories are also, after all, equally complex and contradictory. If we set aside our customarily superstitious approach to religion, seeing it as a legacy that may have something crucial to contribute to current problems and whose engagement does not in any way absolve us of our responsibility to critique it as needed, it may be possible to think the sacred alongside the secular. Here, I contemplate 'dharma' and 'law', allied terms that when thought in conjunction with each other bring to the fore questions that may not otherwise press upon us in quite the same way.

What do law and dharma have to do with each other? Law and dharma are concerned with regulating and mediating personal and social conduct and relationships. Dharma explicitly expresses, and urges us to cultivate, a specific view of life and how it should ideally be lived. Law does this also but more implicitly.

Dharma is often translated as law, duty, etc. It is a term grounded in a Hindu-Buddhist religio-spiritual and ethical framework. The following discussion will draw from this tradition. For my purposes, 'dharma' is living on the basis of the realities of interdependence and the radical equality of all life forms. The notion of free will and the divine 'createdness' of all things are also key here though less relevant in determining the content of what constitutes dharma. Adharma would be living in a manner that contravenes this basis.

Dharma and secular ideals share common ground even though the latter cannot countenance the claim of 'divine createdness'. Law in a secular democracy is grounded in the principles of liberty, equality of all humans and solidarity or fraternity. As an instrument of justice the question of ethics is also at the heart of law. But law is presumed to be fundamentally secular in its orientation. Is it? How might one describe the ethical impulse of law? What is its conception of the human? The same questions may also be asked of dharma but we have a better sense of the answers in this latter instance.

Both law and dharma contain prescriptions as well as proscriptions. The former penalises transgressions; the latter holds out the truth of consequences. Within a Hindu-Buddhist framework, the temporal unfolding of such consequences can take place nano-seconds after the action(s) in question or else be experienced in future lifetimes. What might we learn from the different temporal horizons of law and dharma? What does it tell us about the scope or mandate of each?

The prescriptive function of law is an indicator that morality (understood broadly as 'how one should act') is at the core of its concerns. And yet the content of its normative conceptions is often not directly elaborated but rather displaced onto a notion of 'rights', which becomes the terrain upon which debates proceed. What would we learn if we took a step back and looked at how contemporary law construes what it means to be human? This may provide us some grounds for a comparative contemplation of the ethical visions of law and dharma.

For example, law may see humans as a bundle of rights: the right to life, food, shelter, security, work, etc. Dharma would not conceive humans in this way. It would posit all humans as having been bequeathed the capacity to creatively engage with matter, 'isness', life forms, even transform them. Dharma offers guidelines on how to undertake such transformative activity in a harmonic direction. On an individual level, humans are deemed to have particular tendencies and inclinations and as being vulnerable to certain challenges which they share with the rest of the human subdivision (greed, rage, pride, sense of insufficiency, etc.) Dharma offers wisdom for skilful navigation of these difficulties.

In its most expansive and refined expressions, dharma is about process and principles. It is an invitation held out to humans; a journey to be consciously and *willingly* undertaken. Unlike law, dharma cannot be enforced; nor can its transgression be penalised (although authoritarian tendencies in all traditions pretend as if this were the case). This does not, however, mean that there are no consequences to be borne when dharma is disregarded. Indeed, given the centrality of interdependency to its framework, the consequences of adharma are understood to have repercussions not merely for the individual whose action might have violated dharma, but for the entire collectivity of life forms of which that individual is a part. Each action, whether positive or negative, has implications across human collectivities and across species; in short, for all that exists.

The individual as sovereign subject and repository of rights and duties so familiar in legal discourse is here recast as one life form multiply positioned in a near infinity of relationships. But this does not diminish the importance of individual thought or action. Indeed the intricacy of the interdependent interrelationships that constitutes the whole makes each life, each thought and each action *more* rather than less significant; thus the paramount need for continuous reflection and mindfulness. It is in this recognition of the need to remember that many ritual practices are undertaken.

Within this context legal prohibitions would occupy a local, though not unimportant, place. They would represent a form of social sanction. However, assessment of the rectitude or error of any action would be based on an ethical framework that far exceeds what law can claim for itself.

One may put it this way: dharma is fundamentally affirmative. It is about saying 'Yes! This is who I am, this is how I am connected with other life forms and this is how I must act if I am to honour this truth. And here are some of the personal and social consequences that are inevitable if I and/or others fail to act in accordance with these truths'.

Law is essentially negative. It says, 'No! Thou shall not, or must not, or only in this way and under these conditions is this action permissible . . .' Laws are akin to secular commandments. The affirmative dimension of law is structurally derivative: it is that which is attained when its negative commandments are honoured.

What are the consequences of the absence of an ethical framework other than that which implicitly underwrites law and which brings with it the heavy luggage of a secular modernity? For example, is there a danger that when individuals are seen as a bundle of rights, their dignity as humans becomes contingent on their ability to exercise and enjoy those rights? Is this why secular activist discourse can so often seem to objectify the very lives with which solidarity is being claimed? What moral universes are excluded by the ethical compass of law as a secular institution?

Dharma would contend that dignity is an *inherent* property and that discrimination is the effect of conditioned perception: the result of creating a false hierarchy of life forms that are radically equal and breathtakingly diverse. This focuses our attention on the making of conditioned categories. Law may also concede the social basis of discrimination and posit justice as its telos. But its affirmative dimensions are too closely implicated with its disciplining, restraining function to become a source of inspiration per se. The exception here would be those for whom law itself becomes the ground of subject formation, those whose sense of self and agency is intimately tied to belief in the transformative potential of legal activism. To such individuals law is not simply an instrument. However, few other than lawyers or legal activists can be inspired by law in quite this way. For the rest law-as-morality can only function as antithesis. Thesis: social discrimination. Antithesis: legal intervention. Synthesis?

We find ourselves in a situation in which law is repeatedly being called upon to play a particular version of God: to be the omnipresent, omniscient and omnipotent force policing adharma and fixing all of society's problems whether we are speaking of gender- and caste-based discrimination, corruption or communal violence. But without an ethical social revolution in which beings recognise their mutuality and co-implicatedness, their equality and interdependency, law can hardly be equal to such a task. Indeed, in the present scenario the demand for more law runs the risk of being counterproductive, even regressive. As we have seen, hate crimes legislation or laws attempting to deal with human rights violations can just as easily be used against those in whose interest such laws were drafted. The State and its agencies are after all an integral part of society and as much a part of the problem as they are of the solution.

We may have reached the end of the road of a certain kind of secular strategy, the point at which we see the diminishing returns of what can be achieved by law, or our practice of politics, in the absence of a culturally-attuned moral vision that is integral to both. Our response to the so-called morality of religious authoritarianism and the political right has been to shift the ground of debate to the question of 'rights', whether in its bourgeois liberal variant or in its more inclusive Left and feminist conceptions. However, at the heart of many conflicts is the issue of 'how we should live', posed as a genuine concern quite distinct from the coercive diktats issued by self-appointed guardians of morality and culture. The discourse of rights and freedoms can at best only partially speak to this deeper question.

We urgently need a vigorous public space for discussion of ethics, of a broader framework that can anchor and nurture our everyday conduct and collective imaginings. The lifeworlds of the majority in our subcontinent are sustained by an affective, expressive and complex religio-spiritual epistemology. Failure to seriously engage this reality has undermined secularism's ability to challenge the political theology of the Hindu or Muslim right-wing.

Should secularism turn to dharma to rejuvenate itself? What would it mean to engage with non-secular epistemologies in rethinking law? How might such a project proceed? What would be some key conceptual obstacles we can expect to encounter? How might law derived from secular philosophy be transformed by such a process?

We need to risk such conversations despite the very real possibility that we may have many questions and few answers, false starts and little progress to share. We have nothing to lose but our investment in abstractions whose increasing irrelevance to our collective predicament makes unforgivable any fear on our part to try, lest we might fail.

Note

1. Lata Mani, *SacredSecular: Contemplative Cultural Critique*. New Delhi: Routledge, 2009.

SEX

It may seem odd to suggest that we take a dispassionate view of sex since it has long been understood as instinctual passion. Yet, when erstwhile opponents are united in their conception of sex, only divided in what, if anything, should be done about it, we know we are in the midst of an ideological thicket. In the interests of laying out the problem starkly, if a little schematically, the spectrum may be identified as being occupied at one end by those who seek to regulate sex, and at the other by those intending to free it from such restraints. Placing the issue on a spectrum enables us to concede intermediate positions that offer particular recommendations of proscriptions and prescriptions so far as sex is concerned.

What is it on which all parties are, for the most part, in agreement? Put simply, it is the notion that sex is an irresistible urge and, following from this, that response to sexual stimuli is spontaneous. To some, this makes sex potentially dangerous and in need of disciplining. Elaborate rules are proposed to govern sexual conduct and religious, scientific, medical and 'moral' discourses are mobilised to this end. To others, the fact of it being an irresistible impulse makes it necessary to liberate it from such policing which has historically been unfair in what it has prohibited, and to whom the interdictions have applied. As those who take this position will rightly point out, women's sexuality and non-heteronormative sexuality have borne the brunt of such proscriptions. For it is individuals deemed 'other' by social prejudices like race or caste and practices not approved by bourgeois or feudal morality that have suffered the punitive force of disciplining. Still, whatever their disagreements about what to do about sex, those in favour of social regulation as well as those against it concur in conceiving of it as an irrepressible force. This sets the stage for treating sex as an exceptional realm of human experience.

II

If we look closely at mass media's representation of sexual desire or at debates over sexuality we find that sex tends to be placed in a distinct category. It would seem unlike other phenomena, even those with which it has much in common, like hunger, thirst or sleep. All four are sensory experiences, all impossible to suppress and all are integral to being human. If sex is a physical impetus it should share similarities with other impulses. However, it is unusual to claim that deprivation of food, water or rest inexorably provokes a spontaneous reaction in response. The threat of revolt by the toiling hungry does haunt our unequal societies but the irrepressible narrative seems solely reserved for sex. This conception of sex insists on its biological and thus natural basis and yet sharply distinguishes it from other aspects of the human experience which may also be described in this way.

Unlike food, water or sleep, one can live without sex; many do, whether by their own volition or to meet a social or religious requirement. The prevailing construct would regard sexual abstinence as requiring herculean self-denial. Thus the rolling of eyes and the knew-it-to-be-so-sniggers when those supposedly celibate are found to be sexually active. In its reckoning, to be sexually inactive would imply being repressed.[1]

On the one hand we have the position that announces, 'Sex cannot be left to itself. It must be controlled'. On the other we hear the insistence that 'not only can sex not be controlled, it should not be controlled. It must enjoy freedom of expression'. To those in the former camp, endorsing permissiveness is to risk social chaos (their way of expressing fear of a loss of control — patriarchal, caste, racial, etc.). To the latter group, liberating sex from such control is crucial to the self-determination of individuals. Indeed, sexual self-determination is deemed crucial to the very idea of the modern individual subject and her or his freedom. In other areas of social life self-determination has a different valence; which is perhaps why issues like food security, education or shelter are more frequently spoken of as 'rights' rather than as 'freedoms'.

Sex differs from these other phenomena in one important way: it straddles the domains of need and desire. Acknowledging this fact, however, only raises further inadequacies in the way of thinking about sex we are examining here. To speak of desire — of longing, wish, hankering — is to bring heart and mind into the equation, to liberate sex from an exclusive association with the body. The notion that sex is a primarily physical impulse is called into question.

It is not that the current discourse accords no place to mind and heart in relation to sex. The idea of romance important to the symbiotic relations of mass culture, market and modernity evokes both, but especially the heart. The roles of the triad are mapped in the following way: the mind plans, schemes, imagines; the heart hopes, grieves, delights; the body senses, experiences, releases. This division of labour challenges neither the conception of sex as a primarily bodily impulse nor the narrative structure of sex as release or resolution. Mind and heart, present though they may be in the preparatory stage, are finally upstaged by the body which is conceived as the initiating agent and site of final fruition. The line of causality remains undisturbed.

It will be noted that this discourse is contradictory. It cannot be otherwise for it separates what is integral and intimately connected. To begin with, mind and heart are themselves part(s) of the body and not discontinuous from it. Further, the body is not a physical entity that is capable of sensation but devoid of intelligence. For one thing, sensation is itself knowledge-bearing awareness. For another, awareness as intelligence permeates all three: body, heart and mind. Heart has the ability to plan, body to imagine and mind to feel. Feeling (a term that evokes a depth not to be found in 'sensation') is also a kind of faculty that yields knowledge. To attribute thinking only to the mind, feeling only to the heart and regard the body as the site of instinctual expression is to disrespect the multidimensionality of all three. It is to disregard reality. And it leads to linguistic mayhem, as is evident in the contradictions in my own language as I describe this way of construing sex.

Sex cannot be sequestered as a bodily activity autonomous of mind and heart to any degree. We readily acknowledge this fact in understanding that the trauma caused by rape is not merely physical but also mental and emotional. But this recognition has failed to unsettle the conception of sex that currently prevails.

III

As we contemplate the interconnectedness of mind, heart and body, we are led to discover the limitations of aspects of feminist, queer and Left arguments regarding sexuality, pornography or sex work. The chief target of this critique tends to be the duplicity of the regulatory mechanisms of the state (law, police, etc.), the double standards of dominant society's policing of behaviour and the denial of the right of sexual self-determination to certain groups. In so far as these arguments unravel the hypocrisy of normative notions and the negations and evasions they entail we may readily support them. We may also join in celebrating queer, transgender and women's sexuality. However, to the extent that this intervention shares presumptions with the normative notions it avowedly opposes, it fails to offer a radical reframing of either sex or sexuality. It may succeed in pluralising the content of the normative but it leaves its basic structure intact.

Take for example the exceptional status accorded to sex which is retained in these perspectives. This removes sex from the flow of life activity, severs the interrelationships that constitute embodiment and turns what is a process into a series of discrete practices with a pre-defined terminus. We may distinguish here between Left, feminist and queer representation of sex and of sexuality. The latter is understood as a thoroughly embedded sociocultural practice. The conception of sex, however, continues to retain the sense of an irrepressible natural force notwithstanding the claims regarding its social construction.

What would it be like to think of sex as simply another aspect of life, neither inherently shameful nor intrinsically liberating or revolutionary? What if sex were to be conceived as an ordinary activity like eating or bathing? How might this disrupt the interweaving of pleasure, danger and shame that has long shaped understandings of sex, even casting its shadow on discussions critical of conventional mores? After all, an in-your-face insistence in the matter of sex suggests that, in some way, shame persists as an interlocutor that must be engaged. What would normalising sex in this way do to pornography which depends on the notion of sex as illicit, as naughty but nice?

Sex is a practice that is similar to, and dissimilar from, other life practices. Part of the burden it has had to carry has been the attribution to it of extraordinariness. Social conservatives moralise against it on this basis and sexual libertarians valorise it in response. However, to posit sex as something unique or out of the ordinary is to exaggerate its potential as a source of pleasure and fulfilment; it sets the stage for the promise of sex to remain elusive (perhaps even illusory?). And given the ensemble of ideas that surround sex — from the nature of sexual desire to what counts as sexual desirableness — it initiates a drama of seeking in which uncertainty and disappointment may be experienced in equal measure as pleasure and satisfaction (a cycle that the market economy routinely exploits to its benefit).

To speak of sexual rights without also considering the broader issues posed by our conception of sex is to minimise the challenge before us. Genuine self-determination in sexual matters requires us to confront this ideological formation, not merely settle for insisting on social legitimacy for those persons and practices hitherto excluded. The question of agency is not meaningfully engaged when we limit ourselves to arguing for access to pornography or sex work on the basis of equality or freedom of speech as though these exhaust the issues posed by them. The breadth of what such a confrontation with the construct of sex would involve in intellectual, emotional, cultural, and political terms is a sobering reminder of the interconnectedness of phenomena.

Reclaiming sex as ordinary is far more radical than proclaiming it as revolutionary. To think of sex as ordinary is not to assign it an inconsequential or grudging place but to embrace it as one among myriad life practices in which we may be present to self and other in a loving and reciprocal manner. This would challenge the affiliation of sex with power; with notions of duty on the one hand and valour or conquest on the other. It would also undo the pleasure–danger–shame nexus and the idea of sex as illicit on which it depends. Both have contributed to the way in which a natural aspect of humanness has come to evoke embarrassment; worse, to carry the spectre of immorality.

We need a fresh way to think about sex. Integral to such a project would be honouring the triadic fluidity of mind, heart and body and bringing the awareness of all three to bear on sex conceived as a non-narrative process. To transform sex (and by extension, sexuality) in this direction would require us to heal the alienation that has come to characterise our relationship to our bodies (understood as always already inclusive of heart and mind). Alienation is a state of estrangement. To alienate is to turn away the feelings and affections of someone, of some aspect of self even. The *Oxford English Dictionary* notes that one obsolete meaning of 'alienate' is 'to alter, change or make a thing other than it is'. It seems an apposite description of how we have come to perceive sex.

Note

1. This is not to deny the unskilful way in which many religions handle the issue of monastic celibacy, just to note that within this way of thinking to be sexually inactive would be to live unnaturally.

THE MORNING LIGHT

The morning light
in its piercing delicacy
washes over me
then enters
as if skin and bone
were emperor's clothes
on a fiction we call physicality
But the slowing pulse
quickening blood
suddenly alert mind
belie this notion
And the body is resurrected
in all its sensate glory

WITNESSING

A witness does not merely see. If one wished to invoke the act of observation alone, 'spectator' would suffice. A witness does more than watch an event or occurrence. To witness is to attest to some aspect of what one has seen. 'Witness' has Biblical and juridical roots. That said, the word summons more than subjective perception or incontrovertible evidence. Conceived broadly, 'witnessing' evokes multiple dimensions of that open-ended sense-making process we call 'interpretation'.

II

I remove the black and white prints from the large, rectangular box and lay them side by side on the wooden table: jazz musicians photographed in the concentrated focus of performance. Shot by the Bengaluru-based photographer and cameraman Navroze Contractor, the ensemble represents a lifetime's labour.[1] Most are artists from the US, a few are European and fewer still from elsewhere, Brazil, India among them.

What is immediately striking is the unobtrusive nature of the work. It is as though the photographer is observing a secret conversation between musician and muse. Refusing to collude with the camera's potential to intrude he keeps a respectful distance. He allows the musician the privacy of immersion in creative synthesis. Although evidently in the presence of something unfolding, Contractor does not strive to capture it, take it hostage for posterity. He adopts the stance of a witness.

Contractor's photographs achieve a fine balance. They explore the relationship between musician and muse without privileging either. We do not lose the 'embodiedness' of the performer or the material nature of performance in exchange for some transcendental notion of artistry. Whether it is Max Roach leaning into his drum set, Keith Jarrett's body rising like a treble clef from the piano stool or Rahsan Roland Kirk's forehead glistening with sweat, the musicians are present in all their physicality. Musician and instrument are as one. George Adams' saxophone extends like a limb from his torso. Shrouded in black Tania Maria's piano appears to have dissolved into her womb. Billy Bang's violin billows out of his neck. Even the angular mikes framing Clark Terry seem like musical instruments waiting to be picked up.

The intimate feel of the photographs is heightened by Contractor's decision to use only available light. This makes one peer at them just as one might have at the musicians had one been present at the dimly lit venues. The contrast between the performer, shrouded in an island of light, and the shadows engulfing him or her highlights the enigma at the heart of the genius on display. We may strain to fathom the mysterious collaboration of skill and inspiration. However, we will have to settle for simply beholding it.

The modesty and restraint of Contractor's approach is very effective in this context. Even as we are brought near we are not misled into believing that we are getting inside the mind of the musician. The camera operates as a window not a microscope. We are invited to look and contemplate, not promised we can see and know it all. And as we take up this request we too are infused with the sense of wonder that animates the creative process.

<h1 style="text-align:center">III</h1>

There is an irreducible mystery to creativity. We may know when we are in its presence. We may see it, feel it, sense it, hear it, touch it, enjoy it. But we cannot grab hold of it and subject it to scrutiny until there is ostensibly nothing left to know. At best we can express something of the why and how of it. This is why artists' accounts of their work are narratives of intent, method and process. Of experiments that fail and those that succeed in expressing what impels them. Description prevails over explication. Though artist and critic may seek to explain why something 'works' such attempts are openly interpretive acts, not procedures that dissect and lay bare the object of analysis so that some exhaustive truth about it may be revealed.

The following exchange between jazz saxophonist Zoot Sims and the legendary photographer W. Eugene Smith illustrates this conundrum well. Looking at one of Smith's pictures Sims asks, 'How'd do this, man? Can you explain that to me, how you did it?' Smith responds: 'Yeah, you just pick out your finest solo and tell me how *you* did it'.[2]

We would not think Zoot Sims or Eugene Smith foolish for not being able to explain their achievement. Even those who would rightly resist mystifying the notion of artistic genius would concede that there are aspects that exceed our analytical grasp. We may ponder a piece of art at length, move close to a musician and listen intently, allow the words of a poet to transport us. But something about our experience will continue to elude explanation. Try as we might our reckoning of the work and the pleasure it affords will be partial. Our incapacity in this regard is not, however, likely to unsettle us. For when it comes to art, music, poetry or nature we are accustomed to adopting the posture of a witness, to approaching what is before us with a degree of openness to allowing ourselves to be remade.

IV

What would it mean to extend this orientation to how we make sense of social phenomena? Can witnessing become an analytical approach to the world and our experience of it? The idea of bringing an expansive, exploratory sensibility to how we engage the world may be generally appealing. But it has a particular resonance in the present period in which the art of dialogue appears to have been forsaken. What we see rather is the spectacle of verbal duels in which well-rehearsed positions lock horns. Non-negotiable assuredness prevails over a sense that there might be things that are still to be learned or re-examined, that we may yet be altered by life. Few appear to be besieged by doubts whether on the Right or the Left or the muddled middle of the political spectrum. Meanwhile, outside this zone of proclaimed clarity, social life proceeds in all its ambiguities, contradictions and complexities, and evidence mounts of the insufficiency of dominant perspectives.

Witnessing can bring spaciousness to this discursive climate. As a practice witnessing has received fullest elaboration in the contemplative stream within Hinduism and Buddhism, specifically in the instructions given to meditators on how to watch the mind. The purpose of meditation is to cultivate understanding of the scaffolding of self: how we have come to construe it, the features we have ascribed to it and then naturalised and consolidated through habit. Witnessing is a tool to this end. We learn to watch our thoughts, to gradually notice that we are not identical with them and that there is an aspect of self that observes the recurring patterns that characterise them. A meditator's goal is to become adept at witnessing so as to be able to respond to the world from a place increasingly free of habitual perception.

Among the first things one is taught is to simply observe, that is to say to watch without interfering with what is arising in the mind. This is no easy task. For one quickly confronts one's impulse to continuously edit, judge, assess, add commentary and otherwise interpret what emerges there. All of this usually takes place beneath the threshold of our awareness. The meditator strives to become aware of this process and then to consciously be present to it.

Witnessing brings us face-to-face with our inclination to continually 'manage' our experience. In the repetitive ways in which we undertake this we discover the notions about self and world in which we have come to be invested. As we glimpse the far reaching implications of this tendency to control what we encounter in order that it accord with our convictions, we learn to cultivate spaciousness. We strive to allow things to be as they are, to see where that might lead us and what it might teach us.

An intricate process of disentanglement from habitual structures of thinking and being is initiated. This affords the possibility of apprehending people and phenomena with greater spontaneity and flexibility. We are not promised that conditioning can be entirely shed for it is an inescapable aspect of humanness. What is held out is the prospect of being less constrained by what we believe and as a consequence more able to allow things a degree of autonomy. We gradually learn to distinguish between the incessant flow of thoughts, our responses to them, the frameworks we deploy in understanding the phenomena to which they refer, and the relationship between all this and our comprehension of self and world.

Meditation instructions customarily address individuals and are intended to aid self-understanding. However, as we see, they pertain to the interpretive process more generally. This extends their relevance. We live in a time when a new consensus on social, economic, political, and ecological questions is urgent but appears exceedingly difficult to build. Part of the problem is a hardening of frameworks, a reluctance across the board to allow fresh questions and truths to assert themselves in our consciousness. It is as if we are soldiers on alert, poised to hurl our concepts at our opponents. Witnessing can aerate this dense atmosphere.

Witnessing provides insight into the nature of one's investment in a given position and relatedly to one's resistance to countenance reconsideration. The practice challenges the hitherto self-evident character of our beliefs. As the white heat of certainty cools, all that it currently bleaches or eviscerates can come into view. Developing a measure of dispassion toward our usual mode of understanding permits things in our field of vision to have meaning, purpose and significance that exceed current frames of reference or are external to them. Whether vis-à-vis ourselves or our perceptual apparatus, witnessing sets in motion a process of estrangement from the known that clears the way for fresh encounters and intimacies.

Two processes converge to facilitate a new orientation. Witnessing brings our attention to the inherently relational nature of existence and perception. It helps us to actively experience the fact that the world is not external to us and discontinuous from us; we discover that the world is in us and we are of it. Interpretation emerges as a reciprocal dynamic in which the subject who perceives is constituted in the same breath as the thing perceived. And the thing perceived is regarded as subject in its own right (not merely as object of perception); for the spacious attentiveness of witnessing has led to recognition of *its* beingness, its potential to touch us, to alter our sense of things. At the same time, as described above, we learn to distinguish between the thought, the referent, the framework which gives it meaning, and the aspect of self that observes all of this.

Our growing comprehension of the interrelatedness of things, and our increased ability to distinguish between aspects of perception we had previously experienced as a seamless whole, undermines ways of knowing and being premised on brittle notions of separateness, difference and otherness. We come to realise what such claims necessarily overlook, downplay or deny. As this happens, notions of difference conceived as absolute otherness or else indifferent to relatedness lose their potency to persuade. Not because we see everything as

indistinguishably undifferentiated but because we discover
difference as the play of specificity within interdependent
diversity. Formulations of irreducible difference are revealed
as, at best misperceptions and, at worst, deliberate distortions,
regardless of whether they are deemed natural or socio-
historical in origin, advanced in the spirit of emancipation or
in support of authoritarianism. The relationship of 'ignore'
to 'ignorance' is made evident. And as we begin to notice the
range and nature of the particularities that enliven our natural
and social worlds we are inspired to reach for a more nuanced
language than is to be found in the conventions and polemics
that prevail.

Witnessing remakes the relationship of observing self, subject
of perception and process of knowing into a fluid triad, one
that is continually evolving. The idea of knowledge as capture
gives way to knowing as a form of communing. The sentience
accorded to all things within a Hindu-Buddhist cosmology
supports such a shift. We are led to be curious about the
'isness' of things, to wonder how we might learn to notice it,
learn from it. A space is created whereby surprise, mystery and
accident can assume their place in our understanding of things
alongside predictability, certainty and structure.

V

Can one approach social inquiry as one might a music
performance or a walk in nature? Theorise with the kind of
focused spaciousness that a photographer might bring to her
work? Allow politics to make us contemplative as we might
permit a star-filled sky? How would the politics of difference
be transformed when difference is reconceived as the play of

specificity within interdependent diversity? Such questions could be dismissed as fanciful. But will this response any longer suffice?

Notes

1. See http://www.tasveerarts.com/photographers/navroze-contractor/ (accessed 2 April 2011). The photographs were exhibited in Bengaluru in August 2008 in a solo show titled, 'Listening Camera' at Tasveer. However, nothing compares to seeing the prints. From Contractor's Jazz Series, 23 photographs are part of the Smithsonian Collection, Navroze Contractor Photographs, 1978–1995, Archives Center, National Museum of American History.
2. Sam Stephenson, *The Jazz Loft Project: Photographs and Tapes of W. Eugene Smith From 821 Sixth Avenue, 1957–1965*, New York: Alfred A. Knopf, 2009, p. 151. Between 1957 and 1965, W. Eugene Smith recorded and photographed countless music sessions that took place in the loft of the building in which he lived and worked. The transcribed tapes and Smith's photographs offer a unique glimpse into the New York City jazz scene at the time, ibid.

ON REPETITION

Repetition is integral to learning, to life activity, indeed to
life itself. Breathing is the baseline repetition that ensures our
aliveness. The sun rises and sets with reassuring regularity.
The waves in their unending motion bear witness to the
moon's gravitational embrace of the earth. The rhythms of
our days are comprised of recurrent activities: sleeping, rising,
bathing, eating, working, talking, reading. Yet we frequently
treat repetition as insufferable; as, by definition, boring. Its
positive or neutral meaning as continual, ceaseless, constant
is overwhelmed by its negative sense as interminable, tedious,
monotonous. Why is the idea of repetition so unappealing
when it is a core dimension of everyday life? Has repetition
come to carry some of the weight of our disaggregated
perception?

II

Cows, goats and buffaloes graze in the open field at whose
edge I live. They come every day, in ones, twos or in flocks of
10 or more. They are tended by older women and men who

communicate their instructions with a click of the tongue and a few aspirated sounds; by means of a deft tug of the rope with which some of the animals are led, or else a firm tap on the ground with the stick the shepherds carry. The buffaloes are happy to be escorted but seem to prefer being left alone once in the field. They assume stately postures and move with unhurried dignity. But God forbid that one should be in their path when they break into a run; for a speed matching their bulk is then evident. One watches in awe and not a little fear. Their limpid eyes and indrawn gaze have not prepared one for such a transformation.

Compared to the buffaloes, the cows and goats seem almost domesticated; happy to be grazing in the vicinity of their keepers. Day after day these men and women come; they sit on the mud path or on the grass, under one tree then another. They talk, sew, knit, shell peas and peanuts when these are in season, and spend time in companionable silence. The cows depart at around 3pm, the goats at 5pm and the buffaloes at sundown. One supposes that these rhythms reflect the combined needs of the animals and their human protectors. In the heat, the cold and the rain they take up their positions under an ever-changing sky, filling the air with the sing-song of conversation, the scolding-cajoling of supervision, the high pitch of bleats and bass tones of lowing. To me the scene is comfortingly predictable. And while neither shepherd nor animal convey the feeling that they find their days interminably boring, I cannot vouch for this.

III

'Aggregate' comes from the Latin *aggregatus*, meaning 'united in a flock, associated'. Relationality and multiplicity are integral to this word which signifies entirety, agglomeration, mass, assemblage. The prefix 'dis' when added to a term generally indicates negation or reversal. 'Disaggregate' thus stands for the opposite of 'aggregate', namely, the separation of an interconnected whole into its component parts. It follows that when this whole is disaggregated, the relations of multiplicity and relationality of which it is comprised are also taken apart and remade.

'Taylorism' is a form of disaggregation. Introduced in the early 20th century, it proposed a methodology for breaking down each task or action into timed micromovements in order to optimise job performance and thereby maximise efficiency. Although it is no longer practised in the form initially conceived by Frederick Winslow Taylor, the principle of standardising and optimising work tasks has become the norm in industry. Taylorism met with stiff resistance. Workers found it dehumanising, alienating, soulless. The terms of this critique bear reflecting upon. For although it is conceded that Taylorism carried the division of labour to an unsustainable extreme, many of its presumptions are widely prevalent today, not merely in industry but also outside of it in how we approach everyday tasks and activities.

The nature of the opposition to Taylorism suggests that something more than merely the task is disaggregated when an activity is broken down in this way. This 'something' may be approached by thinking about the kinds of multiplicity and relationality that are negated or severed by it. Some consequences have been well-documented. Taylorism is understood as marking a moment in the history of industrial production when the skill that had previously been the consequence of a lengthy apprenticeship (as had been the case with craftsmen or even 19th-century factory workers) was sought to be displaced by processes that had been determined through 'scientific' experiments as being optimal in their use of time, effort, tools and materials. Once segmented and standardised, each task required less skill and individuals could easily be trained to perform them. The deskilling of workers and their loss of autonomy were inevitable and much resented results.

Subdividing tasks in this way required breaking up bodies and carving up time. It prescribed a rhythm on the basis of which the work was to be done. This measure took some account of the material facts of physicality (for example, Taylor concluded that it was optimal for a worker to lift 21 pounds of pig iron in his shovel and redesigned the implement accordingly). But there was much that it ignored. Bodies were treated as if they were merely tools to be deployed to particular ends. And temporality was construed solely in metronomic terms, as the precise ticking of a perfectly functioning clock. The physical regimen of work mirrored this linear notion of time. This conception of the body and of time was insufficient to the facts.

To begin with, the human body is appropriately conceived not as a sum of parts but as an aggregate of flows, each of which has its own cadence. One may note among others the sleeping and waking phases of the 24-hour day, the altogether different rhythm of the energy cycles of *rajas* (activity), *tamas* (inertia) and *sattva* (alert stillness), our pulse of about 72 beats per minute and the much higher rate at which our neurons fire. Virtually none of these are under our control though we have learned to adapt artfully to some factors such as a tendency to high or low blood pressure, neurological challenges or imbalances that get us caught in one or other of the energy states preventing their natural transmutation and evolution. The Taylorist reimagining of multiply interrelated cycles and flows as discrete linear units capable of manipulation through workplace discipline is, at the very least, naïve.

But the complaint that Taylorism was dehumanising, alienating and soulless implies that something more was amiss. These terms suggest that its methods crucially undermined whatever it was that made an activity satisfying, creative and fulfilling. The process inserted the worker into a predetermined flow external to him or herself. The rhythm of the production line took precedence over the flow of consciousness between sentient labourer and the material with which s/he was working. Labour could no longer be experienced as a communion between human being and the matter being transformed. Simultaneously, the dynamism, familiarity, surprise and unpredictability of this creative engagement was disarticulated in order that the logic of productivity-as-assured-outcome could obtain. It is a sign of the relative newness of the industrial paradigm that workers instinctively recoiled from it as unnatural. They remembered only too clearly what labour could and should be. It is a measure of the distance we have travelled since then that Taylorist ideas in their later incarnations have become entirely normative. What began as a way to discipline the labour process gradually became an orientation to life activity itself. This is the context in which we now commonly consider paid work as drudgery and manual work especially so, associate creativity and self-expression primarily with leisure and the things we choose to do, and think of the labour of reproducing everyday life (cooking, cleaning, etc.) as inherently tedious.

IV

Could this ensemble of ideas be a consequence of negating relationality and multiplicity, the result of undertaking activity in a way that disaggregates its integral nature? There is good reason to propose that this is the case. For the repetitions that reflect natural flows or are congruent with them seem to be those that assure and comfort: the tides, the seasons, the ceaseless transformation of day into night into day. Moving beyond nature into the human realm, activity that honours labour as a reciprocal collaboration and embraces the shifting rhythm of its ebbs and flows appears to manifest spaciousness for actor as well as observer even when it is repetitive, as with *riyaz*, yoga, cooking, cleaning, shepherds at work. However, these same practices when carried out in a way that disrupt or disregard these facts become oppressive and seem interminable. Fulfilment, then, one may argue, is contingent on allowing for a multiplicity of ways, processes and temporalities in how something is done. It depends equally on acknowledging and welcoming the inter-relationships between self and other, self and thing, self and environment, and within oneself between one's body, mind and heart. For our actions express these relationships, indeed are enabled and sustained by them, whether or not we are aware of this being the case.

This complexity is ignored when process is conceived as linked only to product or achievement. Such an orientation paves the way for indifference regarding the conditions in which a process takes place, the basis upon which it is undertaken and whether all aspects of self are present during its unfolding. Additionally, this approach makes no room for the process itself to exert its energy, to manifest its agency and

enchantment, its surprises. Fluidity and mystery are sought
to be corralled into certitude. Time is reduced to a unit of
measurement, emptied of any subjective or natural quality
and labour treated as if it did not also involve the emotional
and sensuous dimensions of intelligence. Is it any wonder that
the consequences are dehumanisation and alienation?

The initial protest against Taylorism grasped something
essential which we who have learned to adapt to its legacy
would be wise to recall. Life is process and actions are the
momentary stabilisation of fluidity as form. To our detriment
we have come to think mechanically of both life and life
activity. Once we have disdain for process then boredom
cannot lag far behind. For tedium is the result of failing to
integrate into the contexts in which we labour, and the means
we employ, the interrelationships which make action possible
in the first place; and which are, in fact, the *sine qua non* of
our ability to sustain it. To blame tedium on repetition is
thus to diagnose as cause something that is only a symptom.
Repetition is a mere feature of industrial mass production.
It is the disaggregating logic of the latter which disrupts
the sensuous flows and multiple rhythms of that activity of
transformation that we name 'labour' thereby undermining
our experience of its inherent creativity.

V

The disaggregation of processes has been further intensified
by technological innovations in the late 20th century.
These have radically enhanced speed and disarticulation
to enable forms of simultaneity and multiplicity hitherto
unimaginable. Technology today is able to swiftly deliver
sensory experiences of varying intensities to large numbers

of people. Multi-tasking has become a near universal feature of life. But more than that, it has become a desire and expectation that many of us bring to virtually everything that we do. Unsurprisingly, the speed, simultaneity and range of what is available as well as our approach to what is on offer make it impossible for us to integrate our experience of them. Sensory overload, overstimulation and dispersed attention are some of what follows. And alongside this, the phenomenon of boredom, loneliness and fatigue especially among heavy users of video games, communication devices, social networking sites and internet-based activities. For the most part users do not relate boredom and loneliness to the modalities of technology (though fatigue is often acknowledged). This correlation is generally proposed by doctors, parents, educationists and psychologists and awaits definitive confirmation by social science research.

The absence of protests akin to the complaints against Taylorism suggests that we have become thoroughly accustomed to a disaggregated way of perceiving and relating to the world. Desire itself has come to be intimately bound up with logics of disarticulation even though these, by their very nature, impede the possibility of its fulfilment. Unable to grasp the underlying reason for our restlessness and scattered consciousness we persist in doing things in ways that continue to impair our capacity to experience the heightened thresholds that we seek. This keeps us locked in a search for ever new experiences none of which quite satisfy. Pleasure comes to be associated with the thrill of the quest and achievement regarded as a temporary resting place in a pursuit without end. The sense of being unfulfilled accumulates and makes life itself seem repetitious and tedious. Over time the two terms begin to imply each other.

A deep and seemingly unsatisfiable hunger for sensory experience is evident today: in the valorisation of sex, the privileging of the dramas of human emotion, the fascination with violence toward self as well as other, and the popularity of things deemed extreme, whether in the arena of sports, adventure, entertainment or life. It is as if we are groping for ways to feel and wish to marshal those experiences as a kind of instinctive protest against ways of being that violate the sensuality intrinsic to existence. This chasing after sensation is a logical consequence of living and acting on the basis of a fragmented perception of things. Indeed the outpouring of affective longings that we currently witness across a range of domains (popular culture, political movements, personal and group aspirations) may be read as attempts to heal the estrangements that flow from disaggregated living. However, to the extent that the root cause of this disaffection is not addressed the assertion of affect is unlikely to be anything more than an inchoate cry. At best it leads to a proliferation of affect-based affiliations or identities, a response that reflects a fractured and partial analysis of the problem.

Reintegration will depend on confronting the logic of disarticulation. This would require us to honour the interrelations (between self, other, thing, environment, body, mind, heart) that we have imagined we can ignore as well as the temporalities authentic to each. We will also need to set aside our romance with speed; to slow down so we can notice and savour our experiences. The natural world can be a mentor and ally in this process; for although its exploitation has proceeded in accordance with industrial rhythms, it has continued to exist outside of industrial time. It can readily remind us that multiple temporalities pertain and need to be respected. To turn to nature in this way is not to evince pastoral nostalgia but to recognise that an integral way of life with all its complex dynamics may therein be observed. The dominant logic of life and work in the post-industrial north and the urban global south has served to obfuscate the real relations of dependent coexistence. The natural world, in its capacity to evoke multiple kinds of interdependence and cyclical time can help us to rediscover and reunite what was rent asunder by Taylorism and all that followed it. This will make it possible to craft life practices that do not deplete or disappoint and pave the way for us to experience our sentient nature in ways that nourish and sustain.

TOWARD DIGITAL DISPASSION

Public conversations on the impact of the internet have
assumed predictable contours. On the one hand the World
Wide Web is seen to have enabled a profound social
revolution by democratising access to knowledge. It is
even considered the harbinger of an evolution in human
consciousness, facilitating as it does new forms of expressive
communication and collaborative practice. On the other
hand, concern has been mounting about the negative effects
of some of these very propensities of the internet to provide
speedy access to vast amounts of visual, aural and textual
material. These pertain to two linked issues: how the web is
designed to operate and the way it tends to be immersively
used (something that cannot be attributed to its design alone).

Concerns expressed throw light on the shadow side of the
technology. One may note the following by way of example:
scattered attention and skimming as a danger inherent to
the exponential potential of file sharing and hyperlinks; the
attendant discouragement of deep thinking; the tendency to
mob-mentality and bullying that is as evident on the web as

creative expression and forms of democratic solidarity; the cumulative, desensitising effects of violent images and games easily accessible via the internet; the at times fraught relations between the virtual and the real (understood either as distinct domains or, more convincingly, as fluid, and interwoven).

The internet has had contradictory effects and there is truth on both sides. Regretfully, however, these standpoints tend to be conceived reductively, as pro and anti-technology positions. Every concern expressed by the latter is countered with yet another instance of the positive use of technology by the former, in turn provoking an example to the contrary. And so it goes on. Disquiet about the impact of technology is also frequently dismissed by referring to past resistance to change. Questions about memory, perception, social relations, cultures of communication and the like were raised in context of the introduction of the printing press, cinema and television. Fears were expressed that each would undermine certain kinds of authority then considered 'legitimate'. It is at times implied that current concerns are equally without merit.[1]

Framing the discussion as a stand-off between those in favour of technology and those opposed to it has evaded the more difficult issues posed by the internet and the cultures of use that have emerged around it. Optimism and scepticism are in an unproductive stalemate. For the most part we have been unable to move toward a critical synthesis that takes serious account of the promise as also the problems that have unfolded in the wake of recent developments in digital technology. We continue to be presented with discussions that shuttle back and forth between alternating viewpoints until time runs out, or else with singular perspectives that do not engage the arguments of opponents.

One might imagine that as an interdisciplinary framework that takes the politics of culture as its object of study, cultural studies, would have been at the forefront of shaping a multi-faceted public debate. But this has not been the case. This may be explicable, in part, by reference to the history of the field. Cultural studies grew out of the commitment of several generations of British Marxists to construing first working class culture, and then mass culture, as significant social phenomena. Their work freed the notion of culture from its hitherto narrow association with elite culture to encompass a whole range of previously excluded aesthetic, rhetorical, discursive, social, and political practices. They advanced a material and historical notion of culture, one indelibly linked to the politics of the social order. Culture was understood dynamically, 'processually'; as a terrain in which both power and resistance were crafted, engaged and challenged. Unlike the Frankfurt School's one-dimensional pessimism regarding modern technological society, it posited sociocultural processes as complex, contestatory and contradictory, admitting the possibility of all three dimensions being simultaneously present.

This conception is supple enough to address questions such as the consequences of exposure to violence, the problem of dispersed and diminishing attention spans and the disjunction between on- and off-line identities, issues that have absorbed clinicians, educators, parents and media researchers. Yet such work has primarily been undertaken with the quantitative and qualitative tools of traditional social science and clinical psychology. These tools have their limitations. They tend to isolate a specific set of factors from their embeddedness in a wider sociocultural matrix than that which defines a given research project. Consequently, even when a finding may accord with one's instinctive sense (for instance, evidence of a relationship between extensive exposure to violence and diminished empathic capacity) it fails to do so in an intellectually convincing way. For the study may have conceived such a relationship in terms more unilinear and less complexly and unpredictably mediated than one might reliably suppose.

Two reasons may be proposed for why cultural studies has not been at the heart of these discussions. First, despite its institutional presence (whether as a free-standing academic unit or as a critical cluster within disciplinary departments) its anti-establishment orientation means that it does not enjoy the status of the traditional disciplines that inform mainstream perspectives. Its ability to shape public debates is accordingly circumscribed. Second, in context of the ignorance, incomprehension, even pathological view of youth and popular culture held by the mainstream, many cultural studies scholars have found it important to explicate the logic, artistry and genius of such expressions. Analysts have pointed to the socio-political basis of contemporary artistic production, its creative and critical retellings of past and present and the kinds of oppositional practices and subjectivities it embodies (the scholarship on hip hop and, in a different way, some of the work on Indian cinema are vibrant examples). Such work has also challenged as needed the racial, gender, sexual and national politics of cultural production. A similar view has prevailed in relation to the place and use of the internet and allied communications technologies.

This tendency to draw attention to the vitality and resistant possibilities of contemporary culture and technology has, however, led to questions of agency being emphasised over those of structure and domination. We are led to ask why this might be the case. One possible reason is the privileged place that desire and agency have come to occupy in contemporary culture. Desire now represents a rationale unto itself such that summoning it suffices to indicate several things at once. The following statement expresses this idea plainly, if a little crudely: 'Those who choose to be continually wired, play video games or create virtual identities for ourselves/themselves do so for the pleasure of it. We/they are aware of what we/they are doing; it is therefore not merely simpleminded to see us/them as exploited but doing so belittles our/their agency and intelligence'. Desire is regarded as the grease that lubricates the engine of individual agency as it negotiates sociocultural structures. The constraining force of the latter may well be acknowledged by user and analyst alike; but it is likely to be regarded as more than compensated for by the unpredictable and creative misuse enabled by desire.

Within this way of thinking, the terms and mode of one's engagement with technology are not at issue. To the contrary, acknowledging one's entanglement with the object of desire (frequently and approvingly described as 'addiction') is deemed to confer a particular kind of authority and credibility. The pleasure of desire and the desire of pleasure converge to propose one's enmeshment as integral to one's comprehension, to one's ability to make sense of things. The concerns of those who cannot lay claim to an analogous relationship with technology run the risk of being dubbed as the alarmist anxieties of cultural scolds or else as the well-meaning but hopeless protests of those who fail to grasp the inevitability and true significance of these developments.

The 'technology-is-here-to-stay-so-get-with-it' perspective is so normative that those who raise concerns in the public domain frequently do so gingerly, ambivalently, and with some degree of embarrassment. And they frequently conclude with a proud admission of their own addiction to that which troubles them, be it a habituation to being continually online or to micro blogging. Technology fluency, technology dependence and technology addiction have come to imply each other. That one could be dependent on technology (as in the sense of being unavoidably reliant on it) without being either savvy or addicted and still have something to contribute to discussions of the issue would likely be regarded as something of a novel idea.

We need to look not just at what technology is doing *for* us or what we are doing *with* it but equally to what it is doing *to* us. Relatedly, we need to ask not merely how *we* may learn to adapt to *it* but equally how its design may be adapted to promoting a culture of use that builds on its affirmative strengths and minimises its negative potential. And we need to explore all of this alongside other dimensions of social life. The question of how technology is reshaping us is deeply intertwined with other aspects of contemporary culture and it is crucial that it alone is not made to bear the burden and responsibility for broader developments. For technology both reflects such trends and makes its own singular and defining contribution to them.

Refocusing our attention in this way leads us fairly quickly beyond technology as a site of creative self-expression, social resistance and critique, to questions of how human sociality and capacity are best nurtured and sustained. Does the failure of cultural studies to lead in this direction have something to do with its having historically occupied an oppositional stance, one in which its utopian dimensions have remained on the analytical horizon and never elaborated as questions of how we could, or should, live? 'Shoulds' have been associated with the narrow, exclusionary politics of conventional majorities and self-described 'moral' minorities; and cultural studies has seen itself as a resistant force that accedes to neither.

But this way of mapping the battle lines no longer suffices. We need to balance open-minded, unprejudiced appraisal and embrace of technology with robust critique of its disciplining and distortive functions. The permissive, libertarian culture of the internet with its seemingly limitless possibilities does not merely signify infinite prospects. It also complements a neoliberal logic that draws on the discourse of choice and self-expression to promote as 'freedom' our subjection to consumerism, and prior to that our subject formation within a consumption-driven economy. The attachments and investments encouraged and reproduced by this economic order have dramatically reshaped notions of leisure, pleasure, creativity, and what it means to be connected with other humans. For this reason alone any analysis of technology today must offer an alternative ethic of pleasure, sociality, desire, and fulfilment. The affirmative vision and imagination of critique must be made explicit.

The nature of the issues posed by technology today press us to move into unaccustomed territory, that of ethics. The question that haunts parents, educators and social commentators disturbed by the changes they observe among those that spend inordinate time online, or playing video games in which violence is so normalised as to be considered unremarkable, is what kind of human beings we are becoming. Lines of causality may be easier to intuitively discern than establish, and mechanical correlations of the 'apple-falls-on-head-causes-injury' variety cannot and will not satisfy. That said, to evade questions of causality and consequence on account of this difficulty s to undermine the radical impulse of cultural studies.

The relation between subject and structure urgently needs to be rearticulated, that is to say, remade. If cultural studies does not recalibrate its focus it runs the risk of being positioned as facilitator (if not accomplice) to violence, consumerism and the making normative of some of the miasmas on which the exercise of power in the contemporary period depends. And it will have to watch as determinists of various stripes locate the roots of this manifestly sociocultural crisis in our primate ancestors or in claims about our 'neurological hardwiring'.

Note

1. Chad Wellmon takes a refreshingly balanced approach arguing that the Web's perceived break with textual culture is overstated. For example, he points to how the hyperlink is the transposition to the digital world of the footnote of Enlightenment texts and functions in analogous ways to constitute authority. Chad Wellmon, 'Why Google Isn't Making us Stupid ... or Smart', *The Hedgehog Review*, vol. 14, no.1, 2012, pp. 66–80.

THE PHANTOM OF GLOBALITY
AND THE DELIRIUM OF EXCESS

'The IPL version of cricket will be able take the US by storm. It is short, fast-paced, played in the evenings, the perfect format'. The young man is confident of his prediction. I on the other hand am startled by this proclamation. While sport is central to the US national imagination, cricket (even the brisk 20-over Indian Premier League variant) would be less than interesting to anyone save immigrants from the Indian subcontinent, the UK, or other countries where the game has a prior history. His comment sets me thinking.

Discussions of the cultural impact of globalisation by and large tend to be debates between two contrasting perspectives. The first proposes that globalisation is a juggernaut that rolls over indigenous cultures, distorting or destroying them even as it imposes alien cultural practices that support its search for labour, raw materials and a market for its goods and services. A second view argues that globalisation is not unidirectional but rather unleashes mutually beneficial processes of economic exchange and cultural cross-fertilisation. Both positions overstate their case. The latter does so by conceiving of globalisation as a fundamentally positive and benign process. The former in its tendency to focus on the disruptive dimension, tends to neglect the complex specificities and tensions that characterise the process of cultural negotiation and struggle.

Any ideology or framework is characterised by contradiction. What is of interest to the cultural critic is how such contradictions are not generally perceived as such. In an important way, globalisation is supposed to render culture irrelevant. Even as its processes attempt to internationalise products and practices that emerge from particular locations and specific histories, the means of their export involves a simultaneous process of disavowal, and a reaffirmation of what is ostensibly disavowed. On the one hand adopting certain patterns of consumption or certain social or business practices is not deemed akin to becoming American or European. On the contrary, we are said to become 'global'. At the same time, such developments are represented as heralding a particular conception of freedom of choice, technological advance, efficiency, best practices and economic rationality, making the narrative of capitalist modernity normative. The sleight of hand in this simultaneous disavowal and what amounts to its recanting is what enables a young Indian techie to sincerely believe that a new format is all that is necessary to make cricket amenable to an American audience.

Post-1993 an entire generation in the middle and upper middle class has been invited to think of itself as global on the basis of its consumption patterns and lifestyle aspirations. Commodities and activities have become the insignia of belonging. This cannot surprise us since globalisation is a market-driven process. After all, it did not emerge from a collective sense of dismay at our ignorance about each other. If it had its trajectory would have been entirely different.

Form has assumed new significance in the current context of economic globalisation. The ubiquity of the word 'lifestyle' is a potent symptom of this. Within the semantics of globalisation 'style' does not merely function as a qualifier which refers to an aspect of life. Style has come to represent life itself, to determine its very quality. Style connotes outward trappings and their place in one's daily life: cell phones, computers, Facebook or MySpace accounts, cars, clothes, foods consumed, and the like. 'Style' also refers to ways of inhabiting the self so constituted, its habits, dispositions, preferences, and to the manner in which one moves in the world in relation to them. 'Style' is a term that bridges the inner and outer realms of the personal and the social. It is in this context that we are urged to 'live lifestyle' as one billboard for an apartment complex puts it.

Other aspects of form have also gained equal prominence: 'form' as structure, arrangement, format, blueprint, method, formula, protocol. These latter meanings of the term come to the fore in the workplaces that symbolise the new economy — information technology (IT), information technology enabled services (ITES), business process outsourcing (BPO) services — and in the new competencies that those working in them are expected to possess. Here the goal is a standardised, replicable set of procedures intended to ensure productivity by means of facilitating seamless communication via eliminating the noise of misunderstanding. Given the transnational publics served by these companies these protocols are supposed to be 'culture neutral'. Indeed their supposed globality rests precisely in their so-called 'cultural neutrality'. Never mind that these procedures are anything but culturally neutral. We now have the context in which a young person schooled in these competencies can be led to think of form as culture; put another way, to think that access to a culture is the same as access to its forms. For it is by adopting certain *forms* (of consumption, communication, leisure, entertainment, career aspirations) that one lays claim to being 'global'. All senses of the word 'form' are pertinent here: form as form (the shell or outer structure) and form as content as in the blueprint for a successful life, arrangement in one's home of one's furniture, art work, and so on.

II

Globalisation as cultural ideology actively fosters this misrecognition. Everything from education to commodities to sports to health is marketed in terms of some notion of globality which is nothing other than the imagined lifestyle of the upper middle and upper class in the first world. Globality is self-evidently about aspiring to live as though one were rich and lived in New York, London, Paris, Frankfurt or Amsterdam and not as though one were poor or lower middle class in these cities. And since one is aspiring to live in one place as though it were an elsewhere the virtual can attain the status of reality, generating and sustaining illusions about both locales.

It is in this context that we should locate the increasingly frequent and rather odd use of the term 'geographies' in lieu of the words 'place', 'locality', 'city' or 'country'. Geography is that very concrete subject that teaches us about physical features such as land, rivers, mountains, climate, natural resources, etc. In its pluralised form, this now preferred term foregrounds a hitherto repressed dimension of its etymology. 'Geography' is formed from 'geo' (from the Greek *gaia*, *ge* or earth) and 'graphien' (to write). Here are two examples of the way the term is now used in certain quarters: 'Vijay Mallya owns property in different geographies' or 'The company has a substantial footprint in Europe and is looking to expand its operations in other geographies'. In its current usage, the term no longer refers to either a descriptive science or to the physical features of a specified landscape but rather to a mental or virtual location without clear referents, a space upon which things are written. The word 'geographies', like the term 'global', evokes rather than denotes. Its seduction lies in its suggestiveness. The resulting indistinctness is fertile ground for projection and fantasy.

To dramatise this point one need only substitute the rather ephemeral sounding 'geographies' with a named country: Iraq, Venezuela, Sudan. We are immediately brought down to earth (every pun intended) and find ourselves in the terrain of history, culture, geopolitics. While projection, illusion and fantasy are not precluded by such a confrontation with material realities the latter do act to constrain one's imagination from running away with itself. Globalisation is fundamentally an economic phenomenon. Consequently it is hardnosed in negotiating the material realities of the economies and societies it is seeking to enter. But precisely because the economic and sociocultural changes that it initiates are so disruptive it requires an unanchored discourse of globality to mediate its effects.

This discourse is principally about shaping the subjectivity of the generation that is its greatest asset, both as employee and as consumer. It is thus that we have witnessed the valorisation of youth. If this segment of the population and market can be persuaded of globalisation's promise, a significant base of support for its project will have been created. A deterritorialised discourse of globality (being global, feeling global, looking global, acting global) offers such a mode of affiliation. And it does so in a way that relieves one from the burden of having to engage the actual material realities in which one undertakes to enact this new form of being and belonging. We will return later in this essay to the ways in which that which this discourse seeks to repress returns to haunt it, complicating the will to power of a globalising agenda.

If one is said to access globality by means of a adopting a set of protocols or practices then one cannot be blamed for imagining that practices (forms) could be substituted for one another. For once you excise history and culture then all you have are empty forms that can travel and generate novel experiences in new markets: ergo our young man's sense of the potential of cricket to entertain 'United Statesians'. But the matter is really not that simple; indeed matters never are and it is the modes of their occlusion (that is to say the ways in which things are obscured) that interests cultural criticism.

The most obvious point is the absence of a level playing field which means that the Indian engagement with Euro-American forms cannot be assumed to elicit a reciprocal response. After all youth in the West are not being groomed to be 'global'. There is a definite directionality to this process. The next layer of complexity we may note is that globalisation does not inscribe itself onto a *tabula rasa* or clean slate. To the contrary, it enters a complex sociocultural space characterised by hierarchy, diversity and conflict. The processes it initiates can fortify, weaken or regroup these features in particular ways. Equally important, those invited to see themselves as global are not passive recipients of its discourse. They actively negotiate and navigate it in ways that very much take into account local, regional, familial, cultural, political, social, historical, gender, and generational considerations. Their sense of globality is refracted by all of this, however unconscious they may be of this fact.

The new economic opportunities afforded to many in a context where the hold of family over youth has been customary has made freedom and choice a reality, not simply an empty promise of globalisation. At the same time, the speedy emergence of an 'aspirational class' is related to the upper-class penchant for conspicuous consumption that predated globalisation in India. Globalisation has simply extended this experience to the upper middle and middle classes. And the capacity to quickly learn new modes of communication and repeatedly draw on them in a formulaic manner is aided by an educational system and culture which accord importance to memorisation and ritual. For instance, the mode of summarising key facts and figures PowerPoint style as adopted by newspapers today (whether in reporting breaking news or in describing the places to which we should 'get away') easily extends our prior preoccupation with general knowledge per se reflected in the popularity of magazines such as *Competition and Success*.

Culture also shapes our sense that cities like Bengaluru can genuinely lay claim to being 'global' despite improper infrastructure. For plumbing and infrastructure are not integral to our notion of a city. This has everything to do with the history of caste. It is caste that accounts for our continued disregard for any form of hygiene other than personal. Caste also explains why our concern rarely extends beyond the boundaries of our properties, for our dwellings are construed as analogous to our bodies. Everything extraneous to their integrity is of no consequence. It is no surprise that our interest in bathroom fixtures and fittings is not matched by a like enthusiasm or concern for what happens to whatever we pour down our sinks or deposit in our toilets.

What else can explain the indifference to sewage currently erupting onto the lawns and pavements of one of the most prestigious streets in Bengaluru? Everything proceeds as if nothing is amiss: shopping, eating, living, breathing. The Bangalore Water Supply and Sewerage Board simply stands by and pumps out the sewage from particular spots at regular intervals each day. This admittedly extreme example serves to make my argument that it is the tendency toward a widespread distaste for matter in our culture (particularly among the upper classes and castes though not entirely restricted to them) that facilitates our being interpellated by a phantom discourse of globality with a highly unstable relationship to facts on the ground.[1]

A related phantasm exercises severe pressure in that region of the world that we are urged to emulate. Multinational capital, as we know, is not patriotic. Its interests lie in making money however it can and wherever it can. If we in India are invited to embrace our status as global in conditions that are a far cry from the cities of our fantasies, it is globalisation as a threat that is brandished before our fellow beings in the West. Let me take the example of the US. The flight of jobs to

China, Mexico, India and elsewhere is real. But the idea that hard-working former peasants in China and clever software engineers in India have put US competitiveness to shame is simply untrue. What we have here is a clear case of capital seeking a higher rate of return and then unfairly holding those it has abandoned as accountable for its decision.

Certainly there is a crisis in public funding of education and of investment in fundamental scientific research in the US. But the causes for this crisis are to be found in domestic policy and have nothing whatsoever to do with whatever is happening in China or India whose record in both arenas is hardly the reason for their economic growth. The so-called threat posed by 'Chindia' is a red herring deployed by US corporations and politicians. It diverts attention from the fundamental fact that the US remains the largest economy in the world (twice the size of China's economy) but simply lacks the will to galvanise its resources on behalf of the majority of its citizens. So the blame is directed elsewhere. And most US citizens ignorant of the realities in either China or India find this explanation credible. And those who know otherwise deploy the fear it induces to argue for the change they rightly believe to be necessary. In either event the claim gathers a greater and greater veneer of facticity.

Meanwhile, half-way around the world, these exaggerated threats, which are dutifully reported by our media, serve as confirming signs of the promise of globalisation for India. A false sense of confidence gradually takes hold at least among the beneficiaries of neoliberal economic policies. A tickertape of data containing growth rates, rates of return, sales volumes, loans raised, investments made, companies sold or bought or merged, moves constantly across the screens of our minds, televisions and computers. An impression is created that we are a nation on the move. The atmosphere is frequently described as exuberant and optimistic. The idea of India as a soft power to be reckoned with begins to be taken all too seriously.

Even so there are signs that continually point to the instability at the heart of these developments. For example, it is no accident that we keep hearing of growth *rates* and not actual values: a high percentage of a small base — 9 per cent growth on India's gross domestic product (GDP) of $703 billion in 2006 — is hardly impressive when compared to the actual value represented by the 2–3 per cent growth of the US GDP of $11.32 trillion in the same year. Going by market exchange rates, the US economy is more than 15 times larger than the Indian economy (five times larger when measured on a purchasing power parity basis). The per capita GDP of the US in 2006 was $45,000, nearly 17 times greater than the per capita GDP of India which was $2,700 (in purchasing power parity terms) in the same year. Many of those described as industry barons or IT czars by our media would be seen as running mid-sized corporations in the US not to mention the fact that the informal economy resoundingly trumps the IT sector in its contribution to the GDP of India.

We begin to see that the true significance of the facts and figures to which we are continually subjected is not statistical but ideological. It may be tempting to dismiss this phenomenon as simply illustrative of the hyperbole that has come to characterise mass media today. But that would be a mistake. For we would miss how such hyperbole is not just a feature of contemporary discourse but also a symptom of what ails it.

III

Excess: from Latin *ex* (beyond) and *cedere* (to go). Defined variously in *Webster's* as: action or conduct that goes beyond the usual, reasonable or lawful limit; intemperance, immoderation, overindulgence; amount or quantity greater than is necessary, desirable, usable, etc.; the amount or degree by which one thing is greater or more than another; surplus. All four dimensions of the term 'excess' are germane to describing the reality and fantasy of urban India in the current phase of globalisation.

Neoliberal globalisation valorises a culture of excess. Proponents may disagree but it cannot be denied that within its logic one can never have too much of anything, be it money, goods, property, sex, leisure, opportunity. Indeed the promise of neoliberal globalisation is precisely that its beneficiaries are enabled to move from a want of options to a superfluity of them. Freedom is defined as the opportunity to avail oneself of these choices. The aspiration for ever more is naturalised as enlightened self-interest but equally as being in the service of the national economy. By some mysterious process, the cumulative realisation of desires is posited as the means by which the majority will be hauled out of their pecuniary misery. The centrality of desire is tied to the construction of individuals as consumers first and foremost: bundles of wants, needs and desires that the market can fulfil even as it provides jobs and meets an exponentially multiplying demand for goods and services. It matters not that the choices on offer — whether of jobs, brands or media channels — differ little in form or content. Variety is strictly a numerical issue.

To exceed is to go beyond. But what are the lines that are being crossed? The definition of excess marks out several of these boundaries: reason, law, moderation, necessity, desirability, usability. The very values that neoliberal theory claims for itself (its necessity, its desirability, its reasonableness in both senses of the term as logic and intelligibility) are violated by the processes it initiates and upon which it depends. Consider the frenzy in that sliver of society that has benefited from India's embrace of neoliberal economics as also the 'reforms' that have assured corporate profitability. Place it alongside the displacement and disenfranchisement of the urban and rural poor, the crisis in agriculture, the widening of socioeconomic inequality, increased pollution and depletion of groundwater, forests and natural resources. Neoliberal globalisation begins to look like a reckless, immoderate, undesirable and unsustainable path. The signs portending its failure are in the very things it celebrates and, as well, in those matters to which it is indifferent such as its impact on human and social ecology. Concern about the integrity of either arises only if a threat is perceived to its unfettered access to labour or raw materials.

Signs of excess abound in our cities. A sketch of Bengaluru would include the following. Mountains of garbage. Gigantic billboards competing for the driver's attention and obscuring the road ahead. Glitzy malls guzzling monumental amounts of water and electricity. Round the clock movement of trucks and tractors bearing construction materials. Excavators, cranes, cement mixers, hard hats, cloth turbans, picks and shovels. Labourers digging, pouring, laying and smoothing cement, throwing bricks in a rhythmic relay up and down rickety scaffolding. The resounding boom of borewells being dug. Day shifts segueing into night shifts. Tractor trailers laden with dirt, brick, glass and concrete blocks from demolished structures searching for empty plots or lakebeds that will serve as impromptu landfills until someone mounts a serious protest against such illegal dumping. Traffic clogging city streets at the beginning and the end of each day and at many times in between. Road widening, one ways, under passes, overpasses, magic boxes. Lives displaced, livelihoods destroyed, communities rent asunder. Property prices climbing out of reach of the middle classes. Completed buildings lying empty as developers wait for the rates to rise even further. Overdevelopment, overvaluations, overheated markets, overtired and overwrought citizens.

There is a distinct sense that things are out of balance. It is as if the city is in the grip of a fever with the rise in temperature being both literal and metaphorical. Fever: a disease characterised by a rise in body temperature and an accelerated pulse, with impaired functions, diminished strength and often with delirium; heat; agitation; excitement by anything that strongly affects the emotions. The situation that confronts us today brings into relief crucial and neglected issues in urban planning and development: equity, balance, sustainability, limit, restraint, regulation, inclusivity, and most important of all, the specific social and cultural context of our cities.

Neoliberal theory can only address these matters as dictum. It proposes more and more of the same medicine as if there will be a tipping point when its prescription will suddenly begin to work, as if it is not working only because our inefficiency, corrupt political system and culture have conspired to undermined its efficacy. Like all evangelising discourses it remains impervious to self-reflection. Its colossal failures in the past are not seen to indicate the improbability of present or future successes. It sees itself as offering salvation to all who embrace its doctrines. Collateral damage is dismissed as regrettable but inevitable and the urban and rural poor who pay the greatest price are deemed dispensable. Thus, the high priests of neoliberal development in India, Montek Singh Ahluwalia, Manmohan Singh and P. C. Chidambaram, can remain impassive and take no appropriate action even as inflation soars and miseries deepen. Like converts to any form of fundamentalism (market fundamentalism in their case) they interpret all signs as merely affirming the basis of their pre-existing belief.

The ideologues may have dug in their heels but all is hardly lost. Not only is there a groundswell of activism challenging the current development path, but also truth erupting even in the most unlikely of places, the world of advertising. Making exaggerated claims is par for the course in advertising. Fantasy as a narrative strategy for creating desire for a product is also common. But the kind of trafficking in the virtual that we witness in this period is unprecedented. Many advertisements border on caricaturing product, consumer and consumption itself.

I will briefly describe several advertisements and then comment on them as a group.

(a) A woman is waiting on a station platform. Her hair is thick and lush but in a way unreal and only possible thanks to Photoshop. Not one strand of hair is out of place. The train pulls in and then out. She is left so thoroughly dishevelled that it seems as though she has been mauled by something. No train or wind could have produced this mess which is as unreal as her perfectly groomed hair had been to begin with. The man who had been interested in her turns away put off by her messy appearance. The woman is crestfallen. The ad is for a conditioner.

(*b*) The cooking stove is filthy; *unbelievably* filthy — caked with layers of dirt and grime in which one could conduct archaeological digs. It looks as if it has been cooked on but not cleaned for years and that rain, dust and windstorms have been sweeping through the kitchen all the while. The smiling man holds a brand of stove-top cleaner. He demonstrates to the young, middle-class housewife how it will cut through the grease to reveal a shiny white appliance. (There are similar ads for bathroom cleaners in which lots of germs are shown gleefully jumping up and down.)

(*c*) Not one, not two, not 10, but countless mosquitoes swarm threateningly as dusk approaches. A well-known Bollywood actress extols the virtues of a brand of liquid mosquito repellent. Its vapours rise and permeate every nook and cranny of the house. She breathes it in as if it were fragrant incense.

(*d*) A woman brushes past her male colleague. He recoils as he apparently feels the hair on her arm against his skin. From the look on his face it would appear that his arm had been grazed by jute or twine not touched by hair. The woman looks ashamed as she is mocked by his companions. The ad is for hair remover.

(*e*) Umpteen advertisements for cars. All of them shot in what looks like California or Nevada or perhaps Ramoji Rao's Film City-version of these locations. No other traffic, silken roads. And of course, no pedestrians or hawkers, no litter, no traffic lights. Newspaper advertisements for cars simply use unidentifiable first world-like skylines. Not Marine Drive or India Gate or anything that would have sufficed in the old days.

Such television commercials and print advertisements are not exceptional but common. What is going on in them? There are a number of interesting things one may observe. First, whether it is the problem that highlights the need for a product or the solution said to be offered by it, everything about these advertisements is excessive. And, at times, such as with the filthy stove, it is excessive in a way that violates existing cultural norms. Indian kitchens are traditionally clean places. No housewife would allow her kitchen to get that way. Showing a filthy kitchen is thus not necessary as a pedagogical strategy. Other contrasts are equally unwarranted. It is not as if those who purchase expensive items like conditioners are so clueless that it becomes critical to pointedly exaggerate what could happen to one's hair if they are not used.

If the unreality of the cleaner and conditioner advertisements unwittingly seems to point to the virtual (as opposed to the real) nature of the need for these products, those for mosquito repellents or cars express the virtual nature of one's enjoyment of them. I do not need to belabour the point about cars. But as far as mosquito repellents are concerned, it is worth noting that we all know we would suffocate if we did indeed shut every window at sundown and breathe in the fumes as in the commercial. We also know that mosquitoes develop resistance to these chemicals far sooner than we do, which is why they can be seen casually circling the coil or dispenser, much to our dismay. We know this and we know it well. Advertisements explicitly rely on our competencies to read and interpret. How do we understand what is happening?

I would like to suggest that advertisements are simultaneously manifesting and parodying the excesses of our current period. If we look closely at these examples, we notice that the relationship between humans and their social and natural environments is a theme common to them all. This is not surprising since consumption takes place in a social context. The advertisements represent this relationship between humans and their environments in two distinct ways. In one, the environment is benign, a kind of backdrop to the product or activity. The car advertisement would be an example of this. But the benign environment is also the virtual environment. Everyone knows that our actual roads and cities are nothing like what is portrayed.

In the second kind of representation, the advertisements for conditioners, household cleaners, mosquito repellents, the environment is represented in a threatening manner. The threat can come from nature (mosquitoes and germs, the gust generated by a train) or from humans making fun of one's so-called imperfections. In such advertisements the natural and social world impinges upon humans in dramatic and fearful ways. There is a third category of advertisements that is a subset of the first. This is one in which humans triumph over sudden danger — such as a motorbike sailing over a chasm in the earth unexpectedly opening out beneath its tyres. But this stunt is so obviously a visual effect that it becomes a virtual victory, a pyrrhic one.

Such advertisements manifest the personal and social anxieties that have accompanied the globalisation process and the forms of alienation from self and environment that they have engendered. Their excesses are but a symptom of the excesses that have accompanied globalisation's stubborn refusal to take into account the nature of things, whether it is the character of urban spaces, the importance of lakebeds and tanks to water security and rainwater runoff in Bengaluru, or the nature of the human body, its need for adequate sleep or sunlight and its tendency to be a particular shape or size. This failure to take nature seriously (and I am using that term in its broadest sense) has produced a fearful repertoire of representations in which nature itself seems to be out of control and in constant need of being kept in check.

Mosquitoes and germs act in improbable ways. Dirt piles up and solidifies on the cooking stove. One's body, one's hair, one's skin act unpredictably to open one to mockery and shame. These representations build absurdity into the very manner of their narration. Products meet unreal needs in unreal ways or offer impossible solutions to all too familiar problems. Such exaggeration and fantasy is enabled by Photoshop and related software technologies which can manipulate image and sound. Facts make way for fictions.

After all if one actually filmed mosquitoes or germs one would be hard-pressed to find them acting with the deliberate and malevolent intent these advertisements seem to imply. Mosquitoes may bite but only until their hunger is appeased; they are not greedy. And if they are coming in droves it has something to do with changes in our environment related to urban development as is much discussed in the mass media. Germs are a fact of life. But our encounter with these organisms is the natural result of dynamic processes of interaction and co-mingling to which we as humans are a party. Germs do not exist to undermine our health and wellbeing. These advertisements invert the line of causation. In them nature menaces humans.

Significantly, however, these advertisements circulate in a context where events (rise in temperatures, pollution, floods, environmental illnesses) are constantly demonstrating the very opposite of what they portray. There is widespread social consciousness of the roots of current problems in environmental degradation brought on by thoughtless human action and its ensuing catastrophic implications for life on the planet. Such understanding is now a cross-class phenomenon. It is to be found among the middle class which has at times been insulated from awareness of its interdependence on its environment. It is also unsurprisingly evinced by the urban and rural poor whose lives and livelihoods have always required a dynamic knowledge of the environment and the most sustainable means of relating to it.

It is in this context that I interpret these advertisements as symptomatic of our collective anxieties and as instances of social truths unwittingly expressed, even if in an inverted and thus distorted form. These representations do not merely embody what we customarily expect of advertisements, namely, awe and wonder about the products being advertised. They also contain dread. Wonder, awe and dread are the three defining features of superstition. Superstition proliferates during periods of rapid and destabilising change.

Superstition is usually dismissed as an irrational form of knowledge that is opposed to reason and it is frequently exactly that. But superstition can equally be understood as a kind of sense-making effort when prevailing reason has forfeited its claim to being credible, when its explanations are patently partial, erroneous or miasmic. I suggest that these advertisements be read as the superstition of a globalising middle class all too aware at some level of the violence of the project in which it has been enlisted and of which it is a key beneficiary. And given that the Latin root of the word 'superstition' also incorporates the sense of standing over or near a thing, it is perhaps not surprising that its script writers are from the world of advertising, the industry most intimately involved in globalisation's mythmaking.

IV

The seeming coherence of a discourse of globality is premised on disarticulating the real relations between neoliberal globalisation as process and policy trajectory and the material realities it enters, transforms, destroys, or remakes. However, the effort to deflect, repress or deny material facts simply does not work. As with any attempt to dismiss truth, the repressed merely returns to leave its traces even in the *sanctum sanctorum* of the wish-generating dream machine of advertising.

That said, globalisation cannot be adequately challenged unless our politics of resistance also take on the processes by which it produces subjects invested in a particular idea of modernity. The culture of globalisation must itself become one of the sites of counter-hegemonic activism. Curiously, this has barely happened. It is only the Sangh Parivar (the three organisations that comprise the Hindu Right: the Bharatiya Janata Party, the Vishwa Hindu Parishad and the Rashtriya Swayam Sewak) that has periodically raised questions about the deleterious effects of consumerism or challenged BPOs continuing to work on national holidays. But the grounds on which they object are usually themselves objectionable.

We need to articulate a progressive critique that directly addresses the worldview of capitalist modernity because this is what makes it possible for many to not see the violence of the project in which they are collaborating. Such a critique has not been forthcoming because even the Left remains deeply invested in it. The Left's problem is not with this conception so much as with the diminished sovereignty and minimal regulatory and redistributive role assigned to the nation state in a neoliberal regime. The Left is not against capitalist modernity, merely against some of its excesses. This is what explains the role of the parliamentary Left in its alliance with the United Progressive Alliance (UPA) and its opposition to the India–US nuclear deal.

Those who believe this position is insufficient for our present planetary predicament need to articulate an alternative vision. This is already happening, whether in the anti-dam movement, farmers' refusal of genetically modified seeds, the return to traditional farming methods, or the many struggles to protect and nurture the environment. A similar move to affirm the natural and sociocultural diversity of urban areas is also gathering force. On 19 June 2008, a unique event called 'Namma Raste' was organised in Bengaluru by the Environment Support Group and the Alternative Law Forum.

The workshop was organised in the wake of a successful public-interest litigation (PIL) filed by the Environment Support Group and the Citizen's Voluntary Initiative for the City (CIVIC) challenging the way Bruhat Bengaluru Mahanagara Palike has been proceeding to widen roads. The PIL pointed out that there was no public consultation and no consideration of the ensuing impact of the road-widening plan on the lives and livelihoods of those affected, the needs of road users other than vehicle owners, or of the consequence of felling a projected 35,000 to 40,000 trees. In response the

Karnataka High Court mandated that all project decisions be referred to a committee that is duty bound to take account of public views and public interest.

The workshop sought to begin the process of dialogue between different constituencies in need of representation: trader's groups, trade unions, slum organisers, urban planners and non-governmental organisations (NGOs) working on a range of issues, from health and disability to pedestrian rights. The hope was to pull back Bengaluru from its descent into hell in context of the drive to make it a global city. The intent was to articulate a vision of the city grounded in the actuality of its vibrant history, people and subcultures as opposed to the futuristic conception currently propelling official decisions. Bengaluru's heritage and conviviality were honoured for making the city what it is for its residents, not as unique selling points of a putative tourist destination. The contrast with the imaginary global city with its empty streets and superfast highways could not have been starker. It was people who were at the heart and soul of this discussion. Each story spoke to an interconnected web of social relationships and practices.

It is one of the paradoxes of the present that the word 'connectivity' has exclusively come to mean the fastest means of bridging the distance between two points. If the meaning of the word 'geography' was transformed by its being pluralised, 'connectivity' has been altered by being narrowed. But the rush to shrink space and time for a small section of elite has brought death and disability on the road to Devanahalli. The expressway to the new international airport in Bengaluru has split a community down the middle. Lives lie divided. Schools, homes, markets, friends, doctors, families can only be accessed by crossing a highway through which cars hurtle at unimaginable speeds. Upon being questioned about the wisdom of what has been done and the absence of any provisions for pedestrians, civil engineers and others in charge repeatedly invoke the term 'connectivity'. The word stands in for, rather *as*, a rational explanation. Apparently no more need be said. There is no sense of irony that 'connectivity' is equally applicable to the community destroyed by the highway. It reminds us of the power of an abstraction to simultaneously narrow the field of vision and normalise violence. We urgently require a counter discourse to neoliberal globalisation. We need to widen our frames of reference and restore to the centre everything that it routinely dismisses as necessary and legitimate in the pursuit of its version of modernity. Our humanity depends on it.

Notes

* This essay was first published in *Economic and Political Weekly*, vol. 43, no. 39, pp. 41–47, 27 September 2008.

1. For an extended discussion of the disdain for matter widespread in Indian society, see Lata Mani, *SacredSecular: Contemplative Cultural Critique*, New Delhi: Routledge, 2009.

COGNITION AND DEVOTION

In analysing Gandhi's philosophy, Akeel Bilgrami
distinguishes between a cognitive notion of truth and an
experiential or moral one derived from what he describes as
general metaphysical conceptions of the world. A cognitive
notion is defined as the truth of propositions verifiable by
reference to properties that exist in the world independent of
oneself. Bilgrami argues that Gandhi set aside such an idea
since it led to an overly intellectualised relationship with the
world. In its stead Gandhi advanced an understanding of the
world as a place suffused with the sacred. For Gandhi, these
'values' (as Bilgrami puts it) made normative demands on
us and invited us to engage the world on terms that are not
detached or instrumental.[1] This essay contemplates some
of the questions raised by Bilgrami's distinction between
cognitive and experiential notions of truth.

In an unlikely entry into some of what concerns me about
this characterisation I consider devotion in its spiritual sense.
Devotion is generally thought of as a feeling. It is described as
the fact, quality or state of being devoted; defined as reverence,

piety, loyalty, faithfulness. It is from the Latin *devotio*, which means a devoting, a consecrating, from *devorere*: to vow, devote. The secular sense of the term evident from the 16th century onwards retains many of these attributes. It references loyalty or commitment to person or cause that is deemed akin to religious devotion.

But spiritual devotion is not just a feeling state. It is also a knowing, a form of cognition. The feeling expresses an understanding. Of what? Of the relationship between the individual, that which inspires reverence, and all else in the world. Although frequently spoken of in dyadic terms (that of seeker and named or formless divinity, Self, Spirit, etc.), in its wider sense devotion expresses knowledge of a triadic relationship between individual, conception of divinity and Creation. The form taken by this knowing depends on the philosophical frame animating the experience of devotion. It is the core principles of this broader perspective that shape such things as what counts as devotion, its practices and the significance attributed to them. Thus the specificities of Christian devotion(s) and their divergence from the practices of reverence or of making sacred to be found in nature-based religions. Devotion gathers its force and meaning, its very *feeling*, from such knowledge.

That said, devotion does not merely express or instantiate this philosophical structure. While it may germinate and be cultivated within a given philosophical framework, the experience of devotion can exceed its boundaries and cause it to be brought to crisis, even to implode. This phenomenon is integral to the spiritual journey itself. Practitioners and mystics in every tradition have bequeathed to us stories of such transformations which recast understandings of truth even as they deepen devotion. At times what is being called into question by the accumulation of such experiences are the very norms of the tradition; at others times merely the seeker's present understanding of these norms. It is a continual process. And it is one in which agency (understood as self-directed purposive action) plays only a contingent part. As Ruth Frankenberg has argued, these dynamics are more properly grasped in terms of the dialectic of spontaneity and cultivation.[2] One cultivates the practices that ground a given tradition but the process itself gives rise to spontaneous experiences that affirm and/or revise one's sense of self, world, practice, truth, the divine.

What does all this have to do with Bilgrami's argument? It complicates the proposed distinction between cognitive and experiential notions of truth. The experiential or moral notion is also deeply cognitive. Devotion manifests understanding and knowledge. Within Hinduism this point is expressed in the respective ways that the path of devotion (*bhakti*) and that of knowledge (*jnana*) are described. Regarding the former it is said, 'the more you love, the more you know'; of the latter, 'the more you know, the more you love'.

Bilgrami would probably concede the cognitive dimension of the experiential notion of truth. However, his naming insufficiently acknowledges it; indeed depends on a conception of cognition that can only partially integrate it. We will return to this further in the chapter. But, and here we come to a point of divergence, the knowing that devotion represents is not derived, as he would see it, from metaphysical notions that are unconnected with properties to be found in the phenomenal world. In fact, to the degree that devotion is a triadic relationship it actually engages, and is in turn engaged by, properties in the world that are independent of devotee or seeker (just as in Bilgrami's cognitive notion). In context of spiritual practice these properties start to assert themselves in the seeker's consciousness. They do not begin to exist as a consequence of metaphysical presuppositions; rather the seeker becomes increasingly aware of their having always existed and of the factors that have prevented her or him from noticing them. This is why the spiritual journey is often characterised as the realisation of a *greater reality*, with the accent placed equally on both of those words.

Examples of such properties would include the interconnectedness of life, the sentient nature of all that exists, the porous boundary between the realm of matter and that of the immaterial or of spirit, the co-implication of immanence and transcendence. I deliberately combine here notions amenable to a secular perspective with others that would be discomfiting or inimical to it in order to acknowledge that the modalities, pleasures and challenges of a spiritual way of engaging the world can be opaque to those not inclined towards it. This unintelligibility has made it suspect as a form of knowing. Indeed it has led to spiritual epistemologies being considered as belief not knowledge; as comprising convictions that are moreover not usually verifiable by a third party. However, this conclusion merely points to the limitations of how cognition has come to be understood. It is neither an indication of its absence nor of the metaphysical nature of what is known.

Cognition has its root in the Latin *cognoscere*, 'to know': from *co*, 'together, altogether' and *gnoscere*, 'to know'. Process and relationality are built into the term. It evokes the possibility of knowing as an intersubjective process (to know together) and even hints at a collective dimension (to know altogether). The latter suggests that what is known together is knowable together; put another way has some kind of independent existence or materiality that makes it knowable in this way. Its root in gnosis points to forms of knowing not predicated on a presumed chasm between the physical and metaphysical. The etymology summons a spacious conception.

Notwithstanding this, cognition has come to be construed almost exclusively in post-Enlightenment terms. This explains Bilgrami's reserving the word for a specific conception of truth and a particular way of arriving at it even as his work is itself a critique of this epistemology as producing an alienating relationship to the world. The divisions between knowledge and belief or the physical and the metaphysical are sustainable only by means of an artificial rupturing of dimensions that are interwoven. We have already noted how it leads one to treat as belief and negate as knowledge that which underwrites spiritual conviction. By the same token it treats as settled knowledge, not assumption or belief, the notion that the realm of the physical is unequivocally separable from that of the metaphysical, so-called.

Accounts of spontaneous spiritual experiences indicate this latter issue to be equally complex. For one thing metaphysical experiences are also apprehended through sense perception; they are sensory events crucially involving the physical body. Visions are seen, mystic sounds are heard and energies are felt. States of ecstasy are embodied states; the body, heart and mind each in their own way are involved in experiencing and making sense of them. Changes to the physical body can accompany such incidents. It may seem from my description that causality is located outside the body while its effects are experienced within it. This is not always so. To continue with the example of devotion, within a theistic framework, longing for the divine can appear to arise from within, seemingly in response to a call from without. But the experience of longing can dissolve this boundary even as, in an apparent paradox, its intensity heightens awareness of one's physicality. Thus it is that spiritual communion is described as a state of mutual giving and receiving, of one as two and two as one. Such union expresses the intimacy of transcendence, the immanence of the supposedly metaphysical.

This is not an argument against making distinctions which are, as we know, intrinsic to semiosis, or the making of meaning. Nor do I mean to suggest that complicated conceptual issues can be linguistically resolved through word play. My endeavour is to register the loss of subtlety that flows from the hierarchy of forms of knowing that we have come to take as normative and the conceiving as mutually exclusive of the physical and the metaphysical on which it depends. With regard to the latter point a further clarification is necessary.

The truth of the claim regarding the interweaving of the physical and the metaphysical does not depend on it being experienced consciously any more than is the case with claims we regard as scientific. In both cases veracity is independent of whether or not a person knows it or knowingly experiences it. What spiritual cultivation makes possible is the *knowability* of this interweaving. Where it diverges from the protocols of an objectivity we have named as scientific is in the process by which one comes to know it and the means of its demonstrability. Spiritual practice holds the potential for a gradual realisation of spiritual truths. Practice can transform *a prioris* into understanding and knowing. If the spirit of this process is to be honoured others can only be invited to consider these propositions, to contemplate them in context of their practice and be free to arrive at their own conclusions. Thus, it is that such knowledge once integrated is generally conveyed as philosophy, poetry or accounts of experience and experimentation. This process of reflection has its own modes of cognition, its own coherence, its own notions of evidence and replicability. And it is one which, in the final analysis, is incommensurable with scientific notions of the same.

The problem then is not that Bilgrami distinguishes between a notion of truth conformable to the norms of natural science and one such as Gandhi's which was derived from a religious framework. The issue rather is the proposed terms of such a distinction. In so far as the presumptions and prejudices that have historically marked secular perspectives on spiritual or religious matters are retained in such a classification it will tend to obscure as much as it reveals. And to that degree the opportunity for a fresh transcoding between epistemes is forfeited. Such a loss would be especially poignant given that Bilgrami's interest in Gandhi is, at least in part, an aspect of his search for a secular basis for re-enchanting our relationship as humans with the world in which we live. If such a process were to proceed on analytical terms that would enhance the understanding of the nature of sacred enchantment it could initiate the kinds of conversation we urgently need to pursue but have no idea how to begin.

Notes

1. Akeel Bilgrami, 'Gandhi, the Philosopher', *Economic and Political Weekly*, vol. 38, no. 39, pp. 4159–65, 2003; Akeel Bilgrami, 'Value, Enchantment and the Mentality of Democracy: Some Distant Perspectives from Gandhi', *Economic and Political Weekly*, vol. 44, no. 51, pp. 47–61, 2009.
2. Ruth Frankenberg, *Living Spirit, Living Practice: Poetics, Politics, Epistemology*, Durham, NC: Duke University Press, 2004.

LIKE THE WIND

Thought arises like the wind
its source unknown
meandering amidst memory and observation
to rest in time
as words on a page
How this squares with the self-knowing subject
laden with value
acting purposefully
upon a world considered brute and inert
is a mystery to me
All I know is that bereft of love for 'don't know'
the metaphysics of modernity
has only suspicion and contempt
for the magical
for all that makes life richly engrossing

INTERDEPENDENCE

Interdependence, like gravity, is a fact of life. Everything
is the effect of our being in a dynamic state of relatedness
and coexistence. Whether we are speaking of the human
subdivision or the natural world more broadly conceived, the
idea of independence is a myth. Yet it is one to which many
humans subscribe. We construe independence as a positive
trait to be cultivated in childhood and regard its coming to
fruition as a defining characteristic of responsible adulthood.
Independence is more than autonomy or self-reliance; it
is a moral virtue that attests to the sovereign nature of the
individual. Not surprising then that any form of dependence
post-childhood can call into question one's dignity and self-
respect, even provoke an existential crisis.

The delusory nature of this notion of independence is
clarified when we look at it closely and alongside its opposite,
'dependent'. 'Dependent' is derived from the French word,
dependre, to hang down, a connotation literally retained in the
word 'pendent'. In the senses most relevant to this discussion,
the *Oxford English Dictionary* defines it as that which has its

existence contingent on, or conditioned by, the existence
of something else; that which has to rely on something else
for support, supply, or what is needed. It would not be an
exaggeration to note that thus far 'dependent' would be an
apt description of the relationship of beings to each other and
of all beings with nature. Our existence is contingent on, and
conditioned by, the existence of things other than ourselves
and we rely upon these for support and supply of what we
need. But there is more; for as already stated 'dependent' is
not a mere descriptor. It is also a relationship that elicits an
unfavourable assessment as in the following meaning: that
which is attached in a relation of subordination; subordinate
or subject.

This negative evaluation comes to the fore in the positive
appraisal of 'independent'. 'Independent' is described as not
depending upon the authority of another, not in a position of
subordination or subjection; not subject to external control
or rule, self-governing, autonomous, free; not depending on
something else for its existence, validity, efficiency, operation,
or some other attribute; not contingent on or conditioned
by anything else; not depending upon the existence or action
of others, or of each other; not having to rely on another for
support or supplies. It would not be an exaggeration to say
that no one can be independent in the ways herein described.

It is interesting to note how the meanings of the two terms
are set out in the dictionary. The entry for 'dependent'
moves from the description of a relationship (reliance,
contingency, conditioning, support) to an evaluation of it.
By contrast, independent is from the beginning not a neutral
characterisation of a relationship but an explicit assessment
of it. Even so there is something odd in the emphatically

negative way in which the term is defined. Each meaning of independent begins with a negation: 'not depending', 'not subject', 'not having to rely'. The repeated repudiation builds a kind of anxiety into the entry absent in the matter-of-fact simplicity of the representation of dependent. It is as if each disavowal is threatened by what it represses and merely serves to underscore the naturalness of dependence, or put another way, of the relations of interdependence.

Dependence signals a relationship, independence the absence of one. As noted above, the relations of dependence are named variously as that of contingency, conditioning, reliance and subordination. Independence, it would follow, is not being subject to such limitations in one's relationships. Is this notion of independence a credible one? Life is predicated on a continual giving and receiving within and across species, through a multiplicity of processes, each of which is in turn embedded in still other interrelationships in a potentially infinite loop. These relationships include those proposed by the dictionary though its definition does not exhaust their range and character.

The dictionary entry may also be said to describe different aspects of the same relationship. Let us take the case of oxygen. Humans rely on oxygen to be able to breathe. Human life is contingent on a sufficient supply of oxygen. Oxygen conditions the possibility and quality of our lives. Following from this it would arguably not be too preposterous to suggest that humans are in a relationship of subordination to oxygen; not in the sense of being inferior to it but in that of being subject to its life-giving properties. One could replicate this exercise for the human relationship with bees. Given their central role in enabling agriculture through pollination our dependence on them may be similarly described in terms of reliance, contingency, conditioning and, in the sense I suggest above, subordination.

There is virtually no aspect of life that does not express a multiplicity of interdependencies and is not itself the effect (contingent and/or conditioned) of such relationships. Everything, whether process or object, human or natural, manifests this principle. The Buddhist concept of dependent co-arising describes this reality as, 'this is like this because that is like that'. Stated in theoretical terms everything is a dependent effect of a dependent cause and each in turn generates further causes and effects in a near-infinite process. This fact compels us to set aside the sufficiency of a single or dominant cause, an approach that erects boundaries around processes that are uncontainable since each aspect of each process sets in motion still other causes, effects and processes.

The words 'potentially infinite' and 'near-infinite' mark the truth that we cannot grasp the social, natural or cosmic whole in its entirety. Any analytic effort can only trace some aspects of the concatenation of cause-effect interrelations that bear on the specific question that it has set out to examine. The omnipotent researcher evincing mastery over his or her object of study makes way for the investigator as modest explorer conscious of the rich partiality of his or her understanding, with analysis understood as an ever evolving amalgam of observation, intuition, informed conjecture and interpretation. Such a researcher does not position him- or herself as apart from the world which s/he sets out to conquer through knowledge but is aware of taking his or her place as a subordinate clause among others in the grammar of the universe.

Given the complex weave of relationships and systems of which the human is but one element, the notion of independence as freedom from constraint is nothing short of a delusion. From this perspective any relationship beyond one's control represents limitation. We cannot then be surprised if relationality itself emerges as a form of constraint! The fantasy of independence is sought to be sustained in one of two ways: by means of an elaborate denial of interrelationships or else via their rearticulation in hierarchical terms. The former leads to the pretence that one's existence can be self-governing and independent of others. The latter challenges this presumption in tacitly acknowledging interdependence but proposing that power over processes and beings can restore the sovereignty and autonomy that these interrelationships threaten to undermine. The valorisation of independence in the current period means that the contradictory nature of the two strategies is not immediately self-evident. It is in this context that the condition of 'being subject' to factors, forces and consequences comes to be equated with a state of subjection.

The laws of the universe do not discriminate between humans, animals, trees, wind, water, fire, stars, planets; in terms of its operation all are radically equal though not all are positioned identically within the whole of which each is an intrinsic part. The idealising of independence as a form of untrammelled sovereignty depends on the elevation of humans as superior to other species and on arrogating to humans the right to control nature and any humans considered inferior for one or other alleged reason. The two ideas mutually reinforce each other. Disdain for those unable to manifest this fiction is an inevitable consequence. Witness the synonyms for the noun 'dependent'. In addition to 'child' or 'minor', these include 'puppet', 'follower', 'lackey', 'flunky', 'stooge', 'parasite', 'underling', 'hireling', 'bondsman', 'serf', 'slave', 'minion', 'vassal', 'servant', 'pensioner', 'grantee' and 'retainer'.

We have exalted a mode of being that is at odds with the preconditions of our existence. The dependence-independence dyad has assumed priority over the *a priori* of interdependence. Accordingly, a life-cycle characterised throughout by interdependence is mapped as a journey from dependence to independence with a lamentable return to dependence in old age. The definition of dependence contains within it many clues about interdependence. But given the privileged status of independence these simply become evidence of subordination, weakness and inferiority.

Restoring our awareness of interdependence involves a reorientation of being even more than of knowing. The sheer scale, scope and complexity of the whole of which we are a miniscule part puts paid to the idea that the world can be brought under some modicum of control by means of 'knowledge'. We may strive to glimpse the various dimensions that constitute phenomena and even comprehend them to a degree more or less adequate to the task that we have set for ourselves. But such knowledge will by definition exclude much that in effect impinges on our concerns but remains beyond our grasp, whether in terms of our comprehension or our capacity to perceive it.

We are not self-governing agents independent of others but beings deeply enmeshed in relations of mutuality of which we are, at any moment, only partially aware. Acknowledging this leads one to discover the *inter*dependence at the heart of all relationships and to rethink the notions of dependence and independence in light of this fact. Both terms assume a greater specificity. Additionally, it becomes possible to affirm the simultaneity of dependence, interdependence and independence. For example, as one acknowledges the dependence of a baby on its mother or a patient in coma on his doctors and nurses, one remains aware that even here there are forms of giving and receiving (of energy if not of goods and services) for which we do not as yet have language or proof, though experiential evidence of such reciprocity is abundantly available. Likewise, as independence is shorn of its moral burden its meaning is made more modest. It signals thinking or action free from coercion and interference though not from influence. This restores the distinction proper between the state of subordination or subjection which is the effect of domination, and that of being subject to forces, factors and processes, a condition intrinsic to our existence.

The understanding of interdependence being advanced here requires that we set aside a hierarchical ranking of life activity. The prevailing view continually resurrects the dependence-independence dyad by considering some kinds of giving as inherently superior to others. To continue with the above example, the mother's care of a baby would be seen to be of greater value than the baby's wordless sharing of its beingness. And the doctor or nurse would likewise be deemed unquestionably more important in what s/he contributes to the comatose patient than anything that the latter might offer by his presence and 'isness'. Such a picture is unsettled by a radical equalisation of activity and exchange. It enables us to acknowledge differences in skills and in kinds of giving and receiving even while equally valuing all. The false hierarchy and painful divide that currently prevails between those who supposedly give and those who supposedly receive is in this process dismantled.

Perhaps the most challenging issue posed by the shift in perspective suggested here is its implication for how we contemplate any action we undertake. We are accustomed to feeling that we can know enough to be able to predict the probable consequences of what we plan to do. This assures us in deciding upon a course of action. This relative certainty is made vulnerable by the idea that everything is the dependent effect of a dependent cause that is itself both the fruition of forces and processes and the initiator of still other forces and processes. To embrace this reality is to adopt a posture of open-minded modesty. We begin by accepting that we can never know it all. Thereafter we develop a scrupulous and heightened attention to that which we know or can learn, and an openness to what may yet remain to be discovered. We cease striving for greater control over knowledge. Instead we aspire to a flexible alertness so that we may take note of what is currently unintelligible to us, allowing it to gradually remake our framework or suggest a new synthesis as appropriate. The aim is not to abandon critical thinking but to ensure that we can encounter people and phenomena in their fullness without our present convictions inhibiting this process from unfolding. Even when the consequence is to reaffirm our current sense of things, it is unlikely that it will not have left its mark upon us, that we will have been untouched. A dynamic interplay of self and other 'isnesses' replaces an instrumentalist and conquest-driven mode of engaging the world. Such an orientation is a logical outcropping of taking interdependence to heart.

RECIPROCAL FLOWS

if giving
is the onward movement
of what has been bestowed upon us
who is the giver
who the receiver
and what is a gift?

donor, recipient
charity, philanthropy
poorly express
the reciprocal flows
by which we are sustained

THE TREE AND I

The tamarind tree stands like a sentinel outside the perimeter of the building in which I live. From the ground its trunk appears disproportionately squat, dwarfed as it is by low, heavily-laden branches. Its crown is level with the third floor and its spread an ample 25 feet. Its feathery foliage is a rich green. It would have been hard to imagine that the fluorescent hue of new growth could acquire such depth with maturity.

Koels and squirrels rule the roost in this particular tree. Other birds briefly alight en route to destinations near and far: sparrows ferrying dry grass for nests, egrets surveying the open field, parakeets abandoning their screeching flight for a fleeting perch. They generally arrive in ones and twos except for mynas who descend upon the tamarind in groups, moving on only after much festive chattering.

The most thrilling of the itinerant visitors are the rosie starlings on their annual migration to the steppes of Central Asia. One of the sublime pleasures of March evenings is the sight of countless starlings spanning the horizon in multiple flocks, the whirr of their wings resounding long after they have flown past. A few occasionally drop away to spend the night in the tamarind. They disappear into its verdant core and quietly slip away before dawn.

But it is the koel and the squirrel that seem to consider this tree theirs. While both male and female koel may be seen, it is the blue-black male with its crimson eye that is by far the more visible not to mention voluble, the flash of its guava-pink throat all too briefly glimpsed when it parts its beak in a cry. By contrast, the brown and white speckled female moves surreptitiously among the branches. When she deigns to make herself visible it is usually on the telegraph wire nearby. The call of the koel is said to herald rain, but these birds seem unaware of this association. Barring the winter when they are silent, they set up their cry at all hours, at times so insistently that it can lead one to wonder what the matter might be.

The squirrels evince less drama although they more than make up for this in flair. Except when eating, they seem to be in perpetual motion, their striped tails perpendicular or parallel to the ground. They can be swift, move briskly or scamper amiably. Something about their manner and alternating pace, their tendency to abruptly switch direction and speed, is reminiscent of Georg Philipp Telemann's compositions for flute. Could the squirrel have been his muse?

The tree offers its sheltering canopy to human and animal alike. Labourers and shepherds rest against its fissured bark; goats, cows and stray dogs stretch out in its shade. A rope hangs from one of the lower branches. Children as well as adults use it to hoist themselves onto the tree in fruit-bearing season. The children pluck the fruit in fistfuls while adults shake the branches vigorously so that the bean-like pods may fall to the ground. These are gathered into sacks and taken home to be shelled though no one can resist sucking a few to savour their sour sharpness. Amidst all this and visible only upon close inspection are ants, spiders and other insects that clamber noiselessly up and down the tree. And beneath the ground, in the netherworld of roots, thrive forms of life known only to entomologists.

The tamarind is visible from my study, living room and bedroom and each offers a distinct perspective. The tree is the first thing that greets me when I push aside the curtains each morning and its silhouette is the last to disappear when they are drawn at dusk. The goings on in the tamarind are a vital part of my daily rhythm. It would not be an exaggeration to say that I live in its ambit. No surprise then that tree has become a site of learning.

II

Observing the rest of nature inspires questions of an existential kind. Something about the beingness of plants, minerals and animals can lead one to revisit the self-evident. The familiar can lose its assuredness, seem vulnerable and contingent. This is not because nature is exercised by philosophical concerns but precisely because it is not preoccupied by them. Post-Enlightenment thought would treat this as evidence of the non-sentient inertness of the rest of nature. By contrast, the capacity for self-reflection would be deemed to distinguish humans and confirm their superiority. Even traditions that concede consciousness to plants, minerals and animals, Hinduism and Buddhism for example, can at times invoke an evolutionary schema in which these are described as lower forms of life. They too posit the ability to contemplate as unique to humans, placing this species at the top of a hierarchy.

Is human sentience radically different from, and superior to, that of the rest of nature? My suspicion is that it is not. To be sure there are specificities to being human, animal, plant or mineral; still it is not clear to me that these are to be understood as they have tended to be. Nothing that I witness from my balcony — the trees, bushes, grass, birds, insects, stones, ant hills — is either inert or mechanically existing. Everything seems rather to be active and related. This is not to say that each exists because of the other, though this may be true in certain instances. Neither is it to claim that it could not be otherwise, that the particular scene is the outcome of some predestined grand conception. Wind, rain, sun, dew, tectonic plates, rocks, soil, animals, insects, birds, humans, etc. have made this landscape what it is. What appears as settled is the effect of multiple, continual processes. What seems old may likely be of more recent origin than what appears new and vice versa.

Some of the relationships between and among what lies before me are evident to me. Others are not either because they are not visible to the naked eye or because I do not have the requisite knowledge. And no doubt there are still other relationships, or for that matter non-relationships, that remain to be discovered by the human and natural sciences. The term 'relationship' marks my sense of the non-randomness of what I observe. It is a way of naming its aliveness, integrity, the prospect of its intelligibility. However, this intuitive recognition rests in the premise that there is much that I do not know and will never know; and in the conviction that much of what we collectively do not know cannot be known unless our notion of cognition is transformed to allow in what is currently not noticed, or is excluded or scorned.

The critique of an instrumentalist view of the rest of nature (in which it exists solely as a resource for humans) has gained considerable ground in the present even though the global economy continues to function on this basis. Although this development has gone a certain distance in decentring humans, theorists have at times continued to prioritise the issue of how *humans* engage with nature. What might it mean to invert the question: to ask rather how we might be engaged *by* nature in ways not of our own making and not an effect of our agency in the sense of conscious, purposive action? What happens when we accord to nature a degree of autonomy, as having the force or energy to cognitively move us in ways surprising and unpredictable? How might we more fully embrace the idea of ourselves as one entity among innumerable others in a web of relationships, movements and flows most of which do not emanate from us?

III

Looking out at the tamarind whilst grappling with a problem has, I have found, often transformed my sense of the difficulty at hand. It is as if something about the tree's existence, its 'isness' if you will, localises my predicament and deprives it of potency. It seems to do this by inviting me to notice that I exist alongside forms of life that thrive on an altogether different basis than the one to which I am accustomed. While I cannot say that I comprehend that difference fully, I can attest to having experienced its salutary effects.

Let me try and illustrate my point with the aid of a meandering example. Like other humans I occasionally find myself contemplating the efforts that can be said to comprise my life. It is, as we know, a vexing issue and not one easily grasped. How do we know the meaning and significance of our lives, our actions? Is significance the same as impact? And how is impact to be determined?

The terms 'meaning', 'significance' and 'consequence' are closely interlinked. The *Oxford English Dictionary* describes 'meaning' as import, sense, signification, interpretation; in generalised use, significance. Significance (in the sense relevant here) is also defined as the meaning and import of something, consequence. Consequence is closely tied to 'significance'. And insofar as significance is also one of the meanings of 'meaning' it pertains to that word too. Meaning and significance overlap considerably and consequence is affiliated with both. However there is nothing to indicate that the former should be comprehended solely or even primarily in terms of the latter.

Yet the prevailing tendency to enumerate, measure and quantify, has led us to routinely conflate meaning and significance with consequence. The larger the scope, the wider the reach, the greater is assumed to be the impact, meaning and import of an idea, action, event, phenomenon, even a life. The degree to which we are heeded, needed, wanted or desired becomes a yardstick of self-assessment. It is not just meaning and significance that are subject to this utilitarian view. Consequence is equally vulnerable. Effects are divided into the tangible and intangible, categories that gather their force from the same perspective.

When impact and magnitude become the measure of meaning and significance, we are led to overlook those aspects of experience and phenomena that cannot be 'quantified' even though they may be vital and integral to them. Conceiving of them as 'intangibles' hardly resolves the problem. It merely fragments the experience further. We may have clearly witnessed and palpably felt these so-called intangibles, for example, the joy and goodwill inspired by generosity or the feeling of spaciousness when in nature. But this does not suffice to challenge their being treated as non-material or insubstantial. The resulting understanding is not merely partial (all knowledge is partial); it is deeply impoverished. It fails to capture the richness of phenomena, of our experience.

Reflecting on the tamarind tree clarifies the limitation, even absurdity, of such an orientation. Does the tree's significance lie in how much fruit it yields? In the number of birds and insects it hosts? In the quantity of carbon dioxide it converts to oxygen? In how many humans and animals seek out the cool of its shade? All of the above? But none of this even begins to grasp the place of the tree in my life (not to mention in the lives of others), the pleasure I derive from its presence, its wordless companionship? Do these facts bear on its significance? And there is a prior question: does the tree's value lie in what it enables, in its function and contribution? Or is the matter of its significance independent of the benefits it is seen to provide? Put another way, are significance and meaning intrinsic to the tree's existence?

When we privilege the quantifiable consequence we value 'doing' over 'being'. Meaning and significance are built around a narrowly construed notion of action: one further subdivided into the more or less significant and by implication the more or less consequential. It is a peculiar framework that makes us more inclined to notice the observable effect rather than the enabling preconditions or the processes that bring it to fruition. Thus our attention is more likely to flow towards the tamarind tree's trunk and branches than towards the thought of its sap rising or its root structure loosening the soil or circumventing a rock as it thickens and extends itself. And we can contemplate our day's accomplishments without valuing the reproductive labour that was necessary to its achievement or the breath that gives us life.

The experiential continuum is carved up into discrete points that index meaning and significance. This process fragments what is, in actuality, a composite whole unfolding as dynamic synthesis. Understanding proceeds by means of a process of continual disaggregation and via the hierarchical evaluation of the inextricable and interdependent. Can we then be surprised if human dissatisfaction has achieved near normative status in our time? Does the existential angst of our species partly express an instinctive sense that something is amiss in how we are led to apprehend the world?

The false distinctions and divides that shape this paradigm are not manifested in the rest of nature. Nature abides effortlessly; it simply is. This is not to say that there is no 'doing', only 'being'. Action is plentiful. But it seems to arise from beingness and to embody a relaxed precision. This is true whether we are speaking of a bird building its nest or one swooping down on its prey; of an idyllic landscape or one being uprooted in a storm. In both examples, the first may be delightful and the second disturbing to behold, but a directness and dispassion cuts across the creative, the peaceful and the destructive. It is humans who are startled and unnerved by this quality in nature, who tend to interpret as 'wrath' or 'revenge' the non-random transformations and devastations caused by the logic of cause-effect interrelations.

The rest of nature evinces a characteristic not frequently observed among humans: it abides non-resistantly, interdependently, in the present moment. Nature is present in a dual, arguably related, sense: it exists in the temporal now and it is always vibrantly alert. This contrasts with the human tendency to dwell equally in the past and/or future and as a result to be less fully attentive to the present. When our distractions and preoccupations confront the 'presentness' of trees, sky, mountain, ocean, fishes, birds, animals, something in us is loosened. Our sense of time becomes more elastic and the compulsions that absorb us lose their grip, their self-evidence. The rest of nature's non-resistance seems to extend itself to us. We are brought into the here and now even without any effort on our part.

The spaciousness we experience in nature is generally considered beneficial to our physical and mental well-being. However, its cognitive dimension is not adequately recognised. (The cognitive is, of course, integral to the mental; my formulation merely accommodates current semantics.) We are not accustomed to regarding the rest of nature as embodying an epistemology, as having the capacity to help humans reconsider how we put the world together. Yet this is precisely the invitation held out by nature's effortless abiding in the present, in a state of non-resistant interdependence.

Living in plain sight of the tree and the grassland beyond it, I constantly confront the difference between my beingness and that manifested by the non-human species outside my window. While I need to work to be in the present, presentness is nature's mode of being. Clarity of perception requires that I be present. But the habitual shuttling of mind between past, present and future impairs my ability to look deeply and see clearly, as do my preferences about how things ought to be. Dominant discourses also fragment my capacity to grasp what is before me, within and around me. I may accept interdependence as a precondition and defining fact of existence. But given the challenging context in which I strive to make sense of the world I am all too aware of the risk of an improper synthesising of what I perceive.

My response has been to proceed cautiously. Every time my effort to think things through generates physical or mental tension I have learned to stop and look outside. Nature invariably extends to my body and mind the gift of its expansiveness. This facilitates a relaxed awareness and one of two things can ensue. New insights or instincts may assert themselves or else I find myself willing to set aside the cognitive task at hand, to allow understanding to unfold at its own pace. It is not that effort is being relinquished; following the rest of nature it is reconceived as cultivating a state of dynamic alertness in which knowing, doing and being seamlessly flow from, and into, each other.

The tamarind, the birds and the open meadow have taught me that nature is more than a source of inspiration. It is an active teacher. It does not merely manifest a mode of being-knowing-acting but transmits it as knowledge to one who is open to receiving it. I cannot say whether the rest of nature is self-aware in the same way that we humans understand ourselves to be. What I do know is that I did not intend to learn from nature; it initiated me as its student. It continually drew my attention to the difference between its mode of existence and mine until that divergence became a site of curiosity and fascination; over time of learning. Could nature beckon me, extend to me its spaciousness, and offer me the example of its own beingness if it were inert and without awareness?

Nature could only commune with me because I allowed it to. My receptivity was crucial to my instruction. I know this because as a graduate student I had lived at the edge of a redwood forest. Immersed in the world of books I rarely noticed the trees except to regret that they let in very little light and were home only to blue jays and banana slugs, a sign, I concluded, of the redwoods' lack of hospitality! The trees lived their lives and I mine. We were neighbours who did not even share a nodding acquaintance. I do not know what opportunity for learning was forfeited.

We are used to the notion that nature evokes feeling, sensation, emotion. The idea that it can also impart understanding, knowledge, wisdom is not as widely acknowledged. Heeding the call of nature dissolves a strict divide between the affective and the cognitive. I 'felt' my way into another kind of 'knowing'. One may equally say that I noticed my way into another way of feeling. Either way it enabled a form of learning that went beyond what I had imagined possible. My frame was expanded; the built environment of mental constructs that had loomed over my perception was resituated within a vast landscape and acquired in the process a different valence, a more modest proportion.

Nature's non-resistance is not a passive stance. It is an active approach in which the first principle of action is acceptance of things as they are. Trees bend in the direction of the wind to survive and birds ride air currents to conserve energy. In so doing both actively engage their environment; neither tree nor bird would benefit from resisting the flow of air. Humans have believed we are superior to the rest of nature because we have the ability to change things, not merely adapt to them. The fallacy of this belief and its destructive consequences for our planet has become clear in recent years. We may intervene in nature but we remain integral to it. Thus we have no choice but to endure the consequences of our actions. Our ability to intervene has merely deferred the question of adaptation, not rendered it irrelevant. Cultivating non-resistant presentness can temper human hubris. It relaxes the cognitive hold of constructs that may be obscuring what is before us and enables us to be with things as they are. The rest of nature invites us to be as it is, open, flexible, dynamic, non-resistant. The ease with which we feel restored in its presence suggests that this is our nature also, only we are inclined to forget.

IN THE FORM OF A PRAYER:
RECONSIDERING OUR POLEMICS

I have been invited to participate in a panel on the impact of fundamentalism and communalism at the annual meeting of the Muslim Women's Rights Network.[1] It has been a lively and informative day. A range of perspectives have been aired, from a strictly anti-religion position, to standpoints affirming of religion though critical of particular interpretations, practices and claims regarding it. The exchanges have been polite, only fleetingly combative. But the various points of view have not engaged each other; that would require some shared ground so far as the question of religion is concerned and that does not seem to obtain. So we have generally witnessed serial declarations with the occasional challenge issued by those of a secular persuasion. Like friends who have no intention of forsaking each other, we listen to — and past — one another. Words crisscross the room single-file. They do not stop to embrace, mingle, recombine, in the process generating fresh meaning and new directions.

Every session has gone over the time allotted to it. An amalgam of exhaustion and frenzy characteristic of conferences towards the end of the day is palpable. I know that some women will strongly disagree with what I am about to say. But my hosts have specifically asked me to share the questions about religion that they know have been preoccupying me. I have decided to take matters head on, to structure my comments as a prayer. I begin. Within minutes I am interrupted as the translator declines to render my words into Kannada, discomfited by what the first paragraph might imply about the content of my presentation. I do not take it personally. It is symptomatic of the contested terrain that religion has come to represent. Someone else volunteers and I return to the words on the page before me. Here is the talk, largely as I gave it.

II

My comments today are in the form of a prayer. Prayer means many things to many people. Here I use it to mark the expression of a concern, the asking aloud of a question that is in one's mind or heart. Prayer can express love, hope or desperation, sometimes all three. One generally prays when one trusts that someone is listening. I trust that you are even though it has been a long day already. Prayer for what, you might ask? That we pause to reflect on the understanding of religion that informs secular political discourse. I offer this suggestion for two reasons. First, because we cannot afford to allow our best intentions to challenge fundamentalism to continue to be waylaid by the poverty of our understandings; second, because the secular conception of religion has ironically more in common with the fundamentalist notion than is generally recognised. I know as well as you that fundamentalism is *not* a religious movement but a political one. But in so far as its politics are grounded in claims about religion, we can all agree that the question of religion has to be confronted.

What is the shared conception to be found in the political rhetoric of fundamentalist and secularist alike? Both see religion as central to the identity of those who are religious; other identities (gender, caste, sexuality, etc.) are deemed secondary. Fundamentalists would see this as a positive thing; secularists as negative. Both see religion as something that unilaterally tells people what to do and how to live and act. Again fundamentalists would approve and secularists disapprove. Both conceive of religious practice as uncomplicatedly producing *social* identities: Hindu, Muslim, Christian. As opposed to what? As opposed, for example, to producing lovers, adorers or bhaktas, of Christ, Allah, the Prophet (Praise be unto Him), Krishna, Devi, etc. Neither the fundamentalist nor secular perspective can integrate this latter prospect. To them the effects of practices on the consciousness of practitioners and the question of their social consequences are foregone conclusions. The meaning of prayer, pilgrimage, mass, *bhajan*, meditation, *puja*, fasting is already known. There is no mystery, no journey. All roads lead promptly and directly to Mecca, Jerusalem, Ayodhya, Vaikunta or wherever. And for the secularist towards superstition and delusion. Despite their differing assessments both fundamentalists and secularists concur in interpreting faith as unquestioned, reflexive obedience. In this view, religious practice captures, expresses and certifies religious identity. Subordinated to this logic the individual practitioner becomes the obedient believer praised by the fundamentalist, or the hapless victim bemoaned by the secularist.

This perspective cannot envisage that one can have a religious identity without being a practitioner of that religion in any active or consistent way; many fundamentalists fall into this category. Or practise a religion without it becoming the axis around which a primary social identity is constructed. This would arguably be true of the majority of Indians regardless of religion. Once religious practice is seen to self-evidently consolidate religious identity, then practice can be nothing other than the demonstration and affirmation of religious identity. Its meaning is made singular, flattened of complexity, subtlety and range. This conception satisfies the fundamentalist fantasy of complete control. And fantasy though it may be, it becomes the stuff of secularist nightmares. Every sign of devotion, every *bhajan mandali,* any religious ritual or practice, every church, temple or mosque is to the secularist a distressing confirmation of the hegemony of religion.

Between these two minority positions (and both fundamentalism and secularism are minority positions in South Asia) is the vast hinterland of religion in which the majority actually live. This terrain is rich and diverse; the root inspiration of our intellectual and creative arts. It deeply shapes the way the purpose, meaning and the travails of life are understood; no aspect of everyday life is firmly separable from it. Philosophically ennobling in many aspects, religion is also contradictory: it is just as capable of tearing people apart as it is of binding them together. On the whole, however, the latter prevails over the former or else religion could not maintain its mass character and remain an ongoing source of affirmation and inspiration to so many.

Practitioners manifest a bewilderingly complex array of relationships to religious institutions, practices and knowledges. They can wax and wane in their engagement with them; repose or withhold trust in God, deity, prophet or son of God, priest, *guru* or *mullah*; go through the motions or bring authenticity and intensity to their practice; treat it as a just-in-case insurance policy to back up their own efforts; participate in religious life for the sake of social convention. Whatever the inclination of the practitioner or form taken by his or her practice, it is dynamic, constantly evolving, as personal as it is social, and characterised by unpredictable twists, turns, and detours. Practitioners express the gamut of human emotions and moods in their attitude to God or worship: reverential, open-hearted, sincere, argumentative, insincere, anxious, fear-driven, greedy, instrumentalist. The unthinking obedient practitioner is a one-dimensional projection that exists primarily in the imagination of fundamentalists and others seeking to exert control via religion. Or in the fears of those secularists whose incomprehension of religion makes them vulnerable to wooden interpretations of it.

If it were merely a question of secularists being off the mark the matter would have only academic interest. But these misconceptions have potent consequences for challenging fundamentalism and thus concern us. In the nearly 20 years since the destruction of Babri Masjid by right-wing Hindu groups on 6 December 1992, secularism has remained the privileged framework for challenging fundamentalism. To the degree that this perspective fails to grasp religion as a complex and powerful force in the lives of people it cannot draw adeptly on its enabling dimensions to highlight fundamentalism's marginality to the broader religious landscape. By the same token, so long as the practitioner is disrespected (thought to be a puppet of forces seen and unseen, labouring under false consciousness or otherwise deluded about his or her own self-interest) there can be no solidarity expected from that quarter. The secular critique remains monolingual and unable to build a mass constituency. For the critique of fundamentalism to capture the popular imagination it has to strike deep cultural roots. And this will require a foundational shift in the understanding of religion, a shedding of secular fear and bewilderment. Failing this we risk becoming facile in our analysis, dubbing cultural practices of enduring depth and history as mere evidence of saffronisation.[2]

In some ways the disrespect toward the religious practitioner parallels the condescension toward the poor and working classes that is at times evident on the Left. The formers' so-called unthinking religious obedience is akin to the way the masses are seen to follow community leaders in gravitating to Hindutva due to lack of access to a 'coherent ideology'.[3] Similar arguments are also frequently advanced in relation to Muslim fundamentalism.

Other issues, specific to Hinduism, would also benefit from rethinking. We need to re-examine the way our polemics conflate the history of caste with the history of religion. To be sure these histories are deeply entangled. Religious sanction has been claimed for caste-based hierarchy and religious institutions have practised caste discrimination. However, while the history of religion overlaps with that of caste, it is not identical to it. If it were, anti-caste bhakti movements could not have arisen nor bequeathed to us such an uplifting legacy. The persecution of such movements is also evidence of the social basis of caste as is the treasure trove of devotional literature written by poets of all castes celebrating the oneness of all beings.

Relatedly we need to reconsider the assumption that the religious world of Dalits is external to Hinduism. The presumption of a disjunction cannot make sense of the diverse threads that interweave to form that complex of ideas and practices that we call Hinduism (regardless of whether some aspects have come to be described as 'classical' or 'great' and others as 'folk' or 'popular'). It may be more helpful to think in terms of a continuum. After all, Kabir's wisdom is continuous with Upanishadic insight and despite the variations in versions and interpretations, folk theatre is rooted in the Ramayana and the Mahabharata.

Dalits have been at the very core of the subcontinent's cultural and artistic life: its painters, musicians, story tellers, weavers, craftsmen, actors. Their role in religious life is not exhausted by the circumscribed place accorded to them by a caste-conscious Hinduism. On the contrary, they have been among its most profound philosophers — Chokha Mela, Ravidas, Namdev, Kabir to name a few — responsible, even more than the tradition's venerated texts, for making the spiritual wisdom of the region part of its collective consciousness and common sense. In seeking to highlight the violence of caste exclusion, it is important that our political discourse does not unwittingly re-marginalise the cultural and philosophical significance of Dalits. The similarities, differences, specificities, tensions and contradictions of religious life in a society structured by caste invite our dispassionate attention.

Let me end as I began, with a prayer that expresses a hope. May we accept that in the political circles in which we mostly travel there is much about religion or faith that is yet to be understood. May we open to the possibility of seeing anew, especially in relation to things we have long held to be settled truths. May our hunger for justice allow us to learn what we need to learn so our struggle against coercion does not run aground in the shallow waters of ignorance, habit and attachment.

I thank you for listening.

III

A brief and tumultuous discussion followed in which the adequacy of my understanding of secularism was spiritedly challenged. I sought to clarify and the conference organisers weighed in with their support. But the questions I had posed remained on paper. Religion continued to be the elephant in the room. Imposing, perplexing, singular; a threat to the very idea of justice. Impassioned words traversed the room single-file not stopping to embrace, mingle or recombine, in the process provoking fresh meaning and new directions. And like friends who have no intention of forsaking each other we lingered afterwards, drinking tea and saying we must talk more about all of this at some point, knowing fully well that it was unlikely that we would.

Notes

1. 'Impact of Fundamentalism and Communalism on Women: The Karnataka Experience', Muslim Women's Rights Network Meeting, Vimochana, 28 May 2011, Bengaluru.

2. 'Saffronisation' is the term that has come to describe the concerted effort of right-wing Hindu organisations to produce a narrative that distorts the history of the region to position as 'outsiders' all but Hindus, especially Muslims and Christians. This movement claims that it is the prerogative of Hindus to dominate culture and society and strives to impose its authoritarian version of Hinduism.
3. People's Union of Civil Liberties, *Cultural Policing in Dakshina Kannada: Vigilante Attacks on Women and Minorities, 2008–09*, Bengaluru: People's Union of Civil Liberties, Karnataka, 2009, p. 3.

AZAN

It came upon us suddenly. Like the roar of silence that dissolves sound and suspends time. Everything paused. Half-syllables of commerce on the cusp of a transaction. Faucets and door knobs about to wrapped. Shop assistants half-way up the ladder. As though someone had yelled, 'Statue!'

'Alla ... hu Akbar ...!' The reverberations slid gently off each surface and crevice to rest with aching slowness upon the sill of our hearts. Waiting to see who would admit the call of love.

The muezzin was in no rush. Longing and hope elongated his sonorous cry. 'Ash-hadu an la ilaha ill-Allah'. Personal yearning purely expressed became a universal summons. 'Hayya 'alas-Salah. Hayya 'alas-Salah'. It was all one could do to remain standing. To not kneel and touch the ground.

The old man across from me was looking down intently, his eyes half-open. The young boy beside him gazed at the chipped nail polish on his hands. Cream was forming on the glasses of tea left untouched on the counter. 'Al ... la ... hu Akbar. Alla ... hu Ak ... bar. La ... ilaha ... il ... l-Alla ... h'.

As the final note faded, the owner of the hardware store coughed. Then said to no one in particular, 'We are Hindus, you know . . .' And the hum of activity was resumed.

HUMAN DIGNITY AND SUFFERING: SOME CONSIDERATIONS

Where does human dignity lie? Is it an extrinsic property dependent on certain conditions? Or is dignity intrinsic to existence and coextensive with it? If one were to follow the general logic of emancipatory discourse today one would have to conclude the former. Dignity is seen to be contingent. Prejudice, discrimination, violence, the economic and sociocultural contexts in which one lives, labours or loves; any of these it would appear can, either singly or in conjunction, undermine one's dignity.

'Dignity' derives from the Latin *dignus*, meaning worthy. *Webster's Dictionary* defines it as worthiness or nobility, high repute or honour, degree of worth, high position, rank or title, dignitary (rare), loftiness of appearance or manner, calm self-possession and self-respect. These meanings ally dignity with social standing and a certain demeanour or appearance. Even if we grant that self-possession and self-respect are not exclusive to any particular social class, the definition strikes one as elitist, as reflective more of feudal and bourgeois sensibilities than egalitarian conceptions considered democratic. The alignment of dignity with location and position is also retained in astrology wherein the term refers to the advantage a planet has on account of its being in a particular place in the zodiac with respect to other planets.

One meaning of the word, however, stands apart from others: dignity as a general maxim or principle. This meaning is marked as obsolete. Lone among the overwhelmingly extrinsic understandings of the term it points us in an altogether different direction. Defunct, discarded, antiquated — such is the current status of the idea of dignity as general maxim or principle. The word 'maxim' is an abbreviation of the Latin *maxima propositio*, meaning the greatest or chief premise. 'Principle', from the Latin *principium*, designates 'beginning'. In the beginning is dignity? Or more precisely, from the beginning is dignity? As maxim, dignity is a concisely expressed principle, precept or statement of general truth; as principle a fundamental truth, a natural or original endowment, an essential element, constituent or quality, the law of nature by which a thing operates. In and from the beginning is dignity.

And yet we have come to imagine dignity as effect, not precondition. Even those who would otherwise reject the conservatism of the dictionary definition can speak, act, exhort and organise as though dignity is something to be ensured, protected, legislated, as if it is something that can be violated. Let us begin with a stark example. We think torture assaults the dignity of the tortured. Does it? However painful, whatever the intention to degrade or humiliate, nothing can touch the inherent dignity of the one upon whom torture is unleashed. The physical, mental and emotional body may be bruised, shattered even, but not the dignity of the tortured. Dignity is unassailable. It is an integral aspect of our very being.

The prevailing view implies otherwise. Take for instance an idea that routinely structures liberal and Left discussions — that workers' rights secure workers' dignity. Such a framing of the issue proposes that dignity is conditional; its possibilities made and unmade by circumstance. This presumption is reflected in the economy of information that supports the activist and researcher in testifying to unjust labour practices and dangerous working conditions. Even when the dignity of exploited labourers is recognised, as evidenced in their manner, bearing or other qualities, it serves to underline the gravity of the need for transformation, not call into question a particular construction of dignity.

As a final illustration, one may point to the regrettably common response to the dependence and cognitive frailty that is at times precipitated by ageing. Family, friends and other well-wishers of those once mentally alert and fiercely independent are often heard to wish for a speedy end to their travails, 'for the sake of their dignity', as if dignity depends on a body and mind capable of self-regulation.

Three interrelated ideas coalesce to shape such a perspective. First, that suffering leads to a loss of dignity; second, the absence of choice leads to suffering and indignity; and third, control over self and circumstance facilitates freedom from suffering and in so doing, preserves dignity. Deducible here is an ideal of mastery over self and context or at least the ability to set limits on how one is impinged upon by social forces and, more broadly, by the conditions of life. Perhaps this is why the feudal lord and bourgeois subject continue to haunt the dictionary definition of dignity. Both figures exemplify self-fashioning.

It is in this context that law comes to be regarded as a privileged guarantor of dignity. Law has the potential to be a great leveller. It offers a means of redress for those not advantageously positioned in the social structure. In its affirmative aspect it bestows and protects rights. In its proscriptive role it penalises their violation. Minimising suffering and maximising dignity come to be identified as critical functions of law.

This discourse normalises the idea of dignity as variable. No longer the inviolable and irreducible aspect of being human, it is conceived as vulnerable to diminishment and by the same token as capable of being enhanced and/or restored. Its ebbs and flows are related to the varieties and quantum of suffering. When suffering is borne with calm resoluteness it is seen as dignified; though when such a stance does not acknowledge suffering it can be read as resignation. However, to respond to trauma with intense emotionality is to risk becoming the object of concern, pity and embarrassment. Anger, aggression, grief, depression or confusion about one's experience can make one the focal point of others' distress about one's dignity.

To construe dignity as something that can fluctuate is to set apart the one who suffers, to propose a gap between him/her/them and others. When dignity is presumed to be in inverse proportion to suffering, those who experience it are structurally positioned as unequal to those in solidarity who have not experienced the same. If in no other way, the tortured individual, the oppressed worker, the infirm human rights campaigner or the one who has been raped is in a state of impaired dignity relative to the activist, the lawyer, the judge or the unaffected citizen who stands in support of them.

The painstaking documentation of suffering necessitated by law and politics further compounds the problem. The marshalling of particulars is essential to making suffering socially, politically, legally, and culturally legible and thus actionable. Details delineate truth and enrich understanding. Campaigns for social justice require that the story of suffering be retold many times over, to awaken the indifferent and disbelieving, to convince police, judges and other interlocutors, to raise funds, to keep the issue alive in city after city, year after year. Affected individuals and communities are centrally involved in these processes.

Testifying to truth in this way empowers the one who has suffered and makes difficult the wilful forgetting of events and realities as some might prefer. However, given the proposed relationship between suffering and dignity, the individual or community in question can come to be seen as indelibly marked by his/her/its experience of suffering. Their lives can dissolve into its narrative. If suffering negatively impacts one's dignity, then indignity can easily attach to one who has experienced suffering. Relatedly inequitable circumstances can transform into undignified ones, and shameful events into ones that bring shame to individuals and communities.

Such demeaning of the one who suffers is no doubt unintended. Ironically, however, it clarifies that dignity is not merely contingent. If it were, redressing suffering would simply be a practical matter. It would not lead to embarrassment or shame. For suffering to pose questions about one's worth or identity, it would have to challenge some core quality; dignity would have to be foundational. It turns out that the obsolete sense of dignity as maxim or principle persists after all. But it does so unhelpfully, in a way that enables suffering to cohere as indignity.

We urgently need to remake the relations of dignity and suffering so that their autonomy is fully recognised. Embracing the *a priori* status and nature of dignity is crucial to such an endeavour. It establishes dignity as an invincible aspect of who we are. This frees us to document the many facets of suffering and domination on a basis that precludes diminishing or deprecating those whose lives are impacted by them. The integrity of person and community is made independent of the challenge and horror of their suffering, not modified or compromised by it. Our sense of the external can no longer be confused with our assessment of the internal.

The present asymmetry between the suffering and those in solidarity with them is thereby softened. Sufferers can speak without concern that their words may estrange them from those who do not share their experiences or belittle them in the minds of their listeners. And those in solidarity are spared the discomfiture of becoming inadvertent voyeurs, especially in relation to acts of violence intended to humiliate, such as rape, torture and the wanton destruction of property and personal effects. When dignity is constitutive, it is difficult to construe solidarity as an unequal, charitable relationship. The way is cleared for a practice that more appropriately honours egalitarian rhetoric and commitments. But there is a further obstacle to be negotiated. And this requires us to revisit suffering, in particular its centrality to a left-of-centre imagining of solidarity politics.

II

Upendra Baxi and Toni Morrison enable us to delineate this conception eloquently and succinctly.

[T]heorizing repression ... best ... happens when the theorist shares both the nightmares and dreams of the oppressed. To give language to pain, to experience the pain of the Other inside you, remains the task, always, of human rights narrative and discourse.[1]

Human rights futures, dependent as they are upon imparting an authentic voice to human suffering, must engage in a discourse of suffering that moves the world.

Over a century and half ago, Karl Marx put the notion of human futures presciently when he urged that they are best born when the following twin tasks occur: when suffering humanity reflects and when thinking humanity suffers. I know of no better way to unite the future of human rights to human suffering.[2]

I insist on being shocked. I am never going to be immune. I think that's a kind of failure, to see so much [human atrocities] that you die inside. I want to be surprised and shocked every time.[3]

Baxi and Morrison attribute a foundational place to suffering in how they envision solidarity. They express a view common on the Left. Suffering is fundamental in two ways. First, the ability to sense, experience, describe and never forget suffering is the basis of fellowship with others. Knowledge of the suffering of others is the bedrock of compassion. It is the means by which one demonstrates one's commitment to challenging inequality. Second, suffering defines the subject/object of human rights, the subject/object of our individual and collective concern. It follows that if we fail to grasp the suffering of individuals or communities, we fail to understand them.

It is in this context that Morrison is determined to remain conscious, not become 'immune' and 'die inside'.[4] And Baxi describes human rights work as 'imparting an authentic voice to human suffering'.[5] While he does remark that the theorist shares both the nightmares and the dreams of the oppressed, that turns out to be more of an aside. Baxi's essay like much social justice discourse gives precedence to nightmares.

What are the consequences of making suffering central to the identity of those who suffer? Relatedly, what are the implications of making knowledge of suffering a crucial sign of comradeship? Each of us is more than the sum of our suffering. Suffering may shape many aspects of our life; it may even be that every aspect of our life bears its imprint to a greater or lesser degree. But an account of our lives is not exhausted by a description of our suffering. I say 'we', not because I am presuming commonality with others, but because I would like to pose this question in relation to *ourselves*. If we do this we would notice the scandal of assuming that suffering is pivotal to the identity of the sufferer in the way generally proposed in political discourse.

Could we abide such a one-dimensional perspective with reference to ourselves? For example, would it not be an insuperable burden were Morrison to serve as a continual reminder of the history of slavery to those who seek to not 'become immune' to its legacy? Is this not a potential consequence of her summons? One might counter that Morrison may in any case conjure this history, with its horror and suffering, for many non-African-Americans. Even if we grant this, we are still left with the reality that individuals and communities while not fully extricable from history are not reducible to it either. The past is not simply reiterated in the present, continuities notwithstanding. Past and present interweave in complex ways that exceed the kinds of derivative understandings and reductionist interpretations implied in viewing suffering as a core, unambiguously defining, experience.

Morrison's wish to encounter each injustice as if for the first time articulates a hope widely shared by many committed to social justice. The unfairness of social arrangements, the spurious grounds on which hierarchies are erected, the violence of divisiveness and hostility provoke distress, anxiety and, where privilege creates a chasm between activist and the suffering, an undercurrent of guilt. The internal dilemma is only heightened by awareness of how readily the situation can be positively transformed given political will and a commitment to mutuality. The witness or activist inhabits the turbulent space between potentiality and actuality. The desire to remain ever vigilant is symptomatic of this existence at the threshold of possibilities. That said, can one be 'surprised and shocked every time' as Morrison suggests? Would this not require a peculiar historical amnesia on our part?

Social reality is a potent amalgam. If one wishes to be truly alive and attentive one would have to embrace *all* of it: not just the misery but also the joy, not merely the rage but also the contentment, not simply the drudgery but also the dynamic creativity of each life and community. The politics of solidarity often unfold as if this were not the case, as if in the end it is the suffering that is definitive. Unsurprisingly then, it also flounders on this very point. For even when subordinated groups emphasise suffering to the exclusion of other dimensions of their experience, they are discomfited by similar rhetoric from those outside their community. Such discomfort clarifies the strategic nature of partial self-descriptions and their capacity to demean when deployed by others.

To what extent is the insistence on cataloguing the sufferings of others a measure of our feeling of impotence as witnesses to social inequality? Is the dedication to demonstrating mastery over the details of suffering a displacement of the recognition that we have little control over its reality? Does our knowledge of suffering function to symbolically manage unresolvable social contradictions even as it serves to distinguish us from those seemingly indifferent to discrimination? Is comprehension of suffering the best means of ensuring empathy?

The idea of empathy-via-understanding of suffering is a Judeo-Christian conception. It is the bequest of a theology which rewrites Jesus' murder by Roman officials as redemptive self-sacrifice. As Christianity becomes the religion of the Roman Empire, the crucifixion of Jesus emerges as a privileged theological moment, the event which more than any other in his life proclaims him as the 'saviour', as the one who 'died for our sins'. As a 19th-century European philosopher, Karl Marx was heir to this legacy. When he speaks of how thinking humanity can be redeemed via empathic identification with the suffering masses and how empathic thinking is itself a form of redemptive suffering, he is invoking this inheritance. Elsewhere, he is more explicit. Once again, I cite Marx via Baxi:

Marx ... wrote in 1850 [and I quote from bloodied memory] that the classical saint of Christianity mortified his body for the sake of the redemption of the masses whereas the modern educated saint mortifies the bodies of the masses for the sake of her/his own redemption.[6]

The torture endured by Jesus on the cross continues to cast a long shadow on how we construe the relations of suffering, solidarity and redemption.

The consequences are mixed. For while Christ as saviour can unite within his personhood the trinity (as it were) of sufferer, witness and redeemer of suffering, the human activist or concerned observer cannot. Consequently, these functions become redistributed and a hierarchy comes into play. Thinking humanity is distinguished from suffering humanity. Striving to be saviours, the former is redeemed by empathic suffering. Meanwhile, even when it is seen to be capable of reflection, suffering humanity tends to be defined by the challenge of its material circumstances and its experience of social discrimination. It cannot be otherwise given the place assigned to suffering. The redemption of the subordinated requires their emancipation from suffering. The stage is set for suffering to be conceived as a kind of damnation, for viewing those suffering in abject terms and for guilt and angst among those committed to social justice.

We need to rethink the basis on which we engage each other across the divides that separate us. Revisioning would require several related shifts in perception. The *a priori* status of dignity would have to be restored. Dignity's autonomy from suffering would have to be ensured. Suffering would need to be situated in the web of life, as one facet of the multidimensionality of human experience, with other aspects also significant to its patterning. This would liberate empathy from a near-exclusive association with understanding of suffering and open the door to a subtler notion of attunement. Activist-witness and designated sufferer will be enabled to meet and remake each other outside the constricting frames that structure present encounters. Such a process, if embraced, could evolve a notion of solidarity more congruent with a truly egalitarian politics.

Notes

* This essay was first published in *Economic and Political Weekly*, vol. 46, no. 36, 3–9 September 2011, pp. 23–26.

1. Upendra Baxi, 'Voices of Human Suffering and the Future of Human Rights', *Transnational Law and Contemporary Problems*, vol. 8, no. 2, 1998, p. 149.
2. Ibid., p. 169.
3. Gary Deans, *Toni Morrison Uncensored*, DVD, Beyond Productions and Australian Broadcasting Company, 2003.
4. Ibid.
5. Baxi, 'Voices of Human Suffering and the Future of Human Rights', p. 169.
6. Quoted in Upendra Baxi, 'The Violence of the *Prabhuta* in the State and the Samaj', Keynote Lecture, Critical Legal Conference on 'The Law of the Law in the Age of Empire', NALSAR University of Law, 1–3 September, Hyderabad, 2006, p. 34.

RETURNING TO OUR SENSES

The mind is often likened to a body of water. When agitated to the ocean with its roiling motion. When unperturbed to a translucent lake that registers movement without distortion, and as the ripples subside becomes dynamically still.

We tend to think of the body as solid: a muscular-skeletal frame galvanised by a nervous and circulatory system, working in concert with organs that perform specific functions. But the body may also be described as a primarily liquid medium. It is after all at least 60 per cent water.

A stone tossed into water initiates a chain reaction. Concentric circles on the surface and in the depths the dissolving concave of the water's non-resistant welcome. The stone's journey is never without a trace. Is this not equally true of the impact of stimuli on the senses?

II

The sensory realm occupies a privileged position in market-driven economies. The invitation to consume is at its root a call to experience. To see, touch, hear, feel, smell and taste: ever more things, ever more intensely, ever more frequently. The increased currency of 'more', 'extreme', 'beyond' is linguistic evidence of this. Nothing is ever enough; 'more' always beckons. The ordinary pales against the allure of the 'extreme'. And 'beyond' is a mythic space on the other side of an ever-shifting frontier. What lies there is not always clear. What for instance does the phrase 'beyond luxury' mean? Unimaginable luxury? Extreme luxury? And what might *that* mean? But the phrase is only seemingly incoherent. Its meaning is well understood. It signposts an increasingly shared conviction that it is in breaching sensory thresholds that pleasure is to be experienced.

The more-extreme-beyond triad represents a construct of sensory experience that has become potent in the present period. The depth, intensity and surprise of pleasure are seen to hinge on challenging limits. Anterior to this boundary is the mundane and ordinary; beyond it excitement and exhilaration. Pleasure is seen to be the product of a chase; one which constantly requires breaking the sense barrier in experiencing something more or different. There are several means to this end: increasing one's consumption of that which brings pleasure (food, drink, clothes, gadgets, entertainment, sex, adventure); trying out contemporary make-overs of older modes of recreation (Bikram Yoga, full-service outdoor expeditions); experiencing new forms of enjoyment (endurance sports, smart phones, social media). The stretching and breaking of limits is an ideal; it is believed that creativity and self-expression lie beyond it. This notion is at the heart of market rationale and is today normative. Many celebrate escalating consumption as a 'natural' sign of economic progress. Who, it is asked, would not want more choice and opportunity?

When we contemplate this conception we observe a contradiction and a reversal. On the one hand is the long-standing and still-prevailing idea that one pursues pleasure to satisfy the senses. However, it is now being argued that to really experience pleasure one needs to go beyond the senses, at the very least beyond one's current experience of them. This positions the senses as mere receptors. The senses become subordinate to a concept of pleasure; a medium in a process that is supposedly about *their* insatiable appetite. As the claim goes, who would not want more choice and opportunity? There is an irony here. Without the senses there would be no pleasure. It is the senses that enable us to experience light, sound, taste, sensation, emotion, indeed life itself. Yet that which is the *sine qua non* (literally 'without which not') becomes that which must be exceeded, extended, tested, provoked, even tricked via the simulation of experience, so that pleasure may be felt.

The relationship between pleasure and the senses is in the process reconceived. From being the consequence of a satisfactory sensory experience, pleasure becomes that which mobilises the sensory realm. The senses become raw material for the operation of pleasure. A relationship of mutuality and intimacy, of pleasure as an expression of sensory fulfilment, gives way to a hierarchical one. Pleasure assumes an *a priori* status, made autonomous. And it dictates a reordering of the sensory realm. What follows is a fundamental reorientation in how we understand both terms.

The logic of this conception leads us away from the senses. It cannot entirely succeed in this since, as already noted, our senses are crucial to our being able to feel anything at all. Therein lies the contradiction. Even so a reversal is set in motion. Pleasure was previously understood as the effect of embracing the senses. It referred to the positive awareness of an experience. It was intrinsically tied to humans as embodied sentient beings. Once pleasure is construed as the effect of going beyond the senses, however, the way is paved for pleasure to become conceptually separable from physicality. We move toward an abstract notion of pleasure. It is not that pleasure has no longer anything to do with the senses; more that the understanding of their relationship is altered and distorted. This remakes one's experience of both.

As pleasure is aligned with the extraordinary it is less associated with the everyday. Even though it is a common experience with quotidian roots, it becomes strongly linked with the uncommon. This is especially true of the kinds of pleasure that are deemed exciting or glamorous. There are countless forms of pleasure and even though not everyone equally enjoyed every kind, the experience has never been considered the sole prerogative of any individual or group. While this remains true, the equation of pleasure with the singular, the special and the unusual promotes the idea that its enjoyment crucially depends on possession of resources and access to opportunity. What are called the 'simple pleasures of life' gradually come to be devalued. And over time they cease to evoke the idea of fulfilment. Pleasure is exiled from the bedrock of life, namely, the everyday. The latter comes to represent the prosaic, the banal, the boring. Dissatisfaction with the commonplace cannot but ensue.

This conception of pleasure also estranges us from our senses, a far more serious consequence. Our senses are forms of intelligence, a faculty with which we are endowed. We rely on them to interpret self, other, our social, cultural and physical environments. Thus it is that the word 'sense' stands for feeling as well as wisdom and good judgement. Sense as knowledge is related to sensation as knowledge acquired through sense-perception. Our very sanity depends on paying proper heed to the senses, their needs as well as the knowledge they yield.

It is in this context that sensory deprivation and sensory overload become means of torture. Deprivation can include hooding, blindfolding, sound-cancelling headphones, sleep deprivation, withholding of air, natural light, food, drink, social contact. Sensory overload can take the form of floodlit cells, continual broadcast of loud music and other sounds, physical assault, electric shocks. Both deprivation and overload are intended to drive individuals to disarray, to destroy their mental, emotional and physical integrity. The abuse of the senses as a method of torture implicitly acknowledges the importance of sensory balance to one's wellbeing. The exceptional context of torture illustrates how mind, heart and body are sources of specific kinds of intelligence. It also underlines their inseparability. If torture is a simultaneous assault on all three it is precisely because each complements and supplements the other as a mode of sense-making and it is together that they provide us with the knowledge necessary for an adequate interpretation of our environment and experience.

Sensory deprivation may be relatively rare outside of the context of custodial torture. But the same cannot be said of sensory overload. In the contemporary period, heightened sensory stimulation is virtually the norm in urban areas and in certain societies a more generalised phenomenon.

Not merely that it is an aspiration and objective to be pursued. As we have seen, the very idea of pleasure hinges on the premise of more, better, different, extreme. Even once we grant that sensory overload designed to punish is markedly different from the simultaneous, multiplicitous stimulation that has become the rage and the norm, questions remain. To what extent is the seemingly persistent cycle of hunger for stimulation and dissatisfaction with experience of it, related to a construct of pleasure unmoored from physicality and sensuality as the fundament of embodiment? Is our restlessness to do with the fact that we are in effect being encouraged to take flight from that to which we must pay close attention if we are to enjoy anything at all?

Fulfilment is crucially tied to the integration of experience. To integrate is to unify, to bring together various parts to complete a thing or process. How would we as embodied, sentient beings integrate pleasure? Through the quality of awareness we bring to an experience, the degree to which we are wholly present to it. If pleasure is a sensory experience deemed positive and fulfilment is the effect of its integration, then contentment is inextricable from a conscious awareness of our sensorium. Satisfaction depends on our paying attention to the textures, tastes, sounds, feelings, sights, smells, emotions and mind-states that constitute a given process, event, transaction or experience. It is contingent on mindfulness of our senses. What may once have been self-evident is no longer so. It is paradoxical. Consumerism would appear to celebrate the senses. But it does so in a way that actually disparages them; construing them merely as something to be aroused, stimulated, indulged and outstripped. This contempt returns to haunt it as perpetual dissatisfaction.

The tension between consumerism's promise of exponential pleasure and the fact of discontent and boredom evidenced in the perennial search for new iterations of enjoyment is generally understood by reference to several suppositions. These include the inexhaustible nature of desire, the insatiable appetite of the senses, the essential restlessness of the human spirit and inner turmoil as the precondition and spur of creativity. Such presumptions pre-date the market economy and have a broader cultural provenance; for instance, in the modern notion of the artist as an often troubled nonconformist or in the distrust of the senses that forms an important strand in both secular and religious thought. In the present these assumptions also serve to support the idea that the market is a rational response to the needs and wants of humans. Who, as it is said, would not want more choice and opportunity? What we have here is a mode of reasoning that naturalises then elevates the potential of disquiet and is dismissive of the senses even as it claims to cater to them.

III

One way to break with this logic is to reclaim the senses as a faculty crucial to our ability to experience life fully, its pleasures included. This would chart a way forward that neither exploits the senses (as with the market) nor attempts to discipline them (as with some social and religious frameworks). A third path is premised on embracing the senses. It requires bringing to them a certain quality of attentiveness. We learn to read them in ways we have become habituated to not doing: empathically, dispassionately and reflexively.

Such attentiveness is characterised by an expansive focus. Expansive because the intent is not to concentrate on one aspect to the exclusion of others; focus since it involves heightened awareness. After all we have five senses (arguably a sixth) all of which are in play in each moment and making sense of them integrally involves the heart and the mind. Interpretation is by definition a multidimensional, multifactorial process. But there are constraints. A focused spaciousness on multiple aspects is easier to cultivate in certain contexts. Two contrasting examples may help to clarify the point. A runner is simultaneously aware of multiple things: her environment, her physical and mental stamina, her timing, her thirst, her emotional state, and so on. Her body-in-motion provides the fulcrum for integrated awareness. The multiplicity of which she is acutely conscious is part of a single flow or action, her running. The setting facilitates expansive focus.

Such awareness is, however, much harder in context of activities designed to accentuate particular senses or dimensions thereof. Take, for instance, the thrill of speed or the terror of horror; if the excitingly vertiginous sensation one feels is the result of experiencing speeds difficult to physically and thus consciously assimilate, or if horror keeps one heart-in-mouth-at-the-of- edge-of-one's-seat-unable-to-be-aware-of-little-other-than- what-has-generated-this-sensation, then an integrative attentiveness is simply not feasible. The speed and intensity of the sensory onrush make impossible a conscious integration of the experience. To draw on an earlier analogy, we are here positioned to be aware of the impact of a stone on the surface of a lake but not of its reverberations as it free-falls to the bottom.

An integrative awareness is premised on accepting the limits placed by our embodiment on the kind and quantum of sensory experience we can synthesise at any one time. It distinguishes our capacity to be cognisant of many things (the multiple screens on our computers, text messages on our cell phones, people and conversations around us, traffic noise, physical sensations, a variety of emotional and mental states, etc.) from our ability to cognitively, physically and emotionally consolidate this experience in the way being suggested here as crucial to fulfilment. Awareness as an expansive focus involves not merely noticing multiplicity but also its effects on our reception, perception and experience. One does not strive for omniscience; to return to our analogy, one cannot follow every ripple till it subsides since each will initiate further ripples both on the surface and in the depths. One charts a course between the impossibility of being all-knowing or all-sensing and the insufficiency of merely noticing. Registering stimuli can momentarily thrill but sustained pleasure depends on our ability to integrate them.

The approach being proposed here is at odds with entertainment as it has come to be understood, produced and experienced. Pleasure has become bound up with multiplicity, simultaneity, quantity and speed. Much of it can only be accessed as a non-integrated experience. The very idea of limits is an anathema. However, the diminishing returns of a logic that dis-enables sensory integration of pleasure have also been discernible and not just in the ubiquity of discontent. For in parallel there has been wide interest in forms of experience based on contrary principles: yoga, meditation, trekking, ecotourism, mindful waste management, the slow food movement. These developments have at times been entangled with the very economy and pleasure principle they have set out to question or have the potential to undermine.

For example, alongside the traditional teaching of yoga as a meditative physical practice one has seen its reformulation as aerobic calisthenics. Similarly, the culture of fitness has not usually implied a holistic view of the body since exercise routines and machines often work to disaggregate it. And ecotourism has at times been a branding device with little to differentiate it from the heavy-footprint forms of travel against which it defines itself. Even so, these developments bear testimony to the enduring call of the senses, to the continued attraction of communing with our embodiedness and with the physical world around us.

To return to our senses is to embark on a complex, interpretive process. It requires us to divest ourselves of the ways the senses have come to be crudely understood as a kind of impulse easy to manipulate. As already noted, this view has led some to construe them as sources of peril in need of supervision. Re-conceiving them as forms of intelligence involves two related practices: an unlearning of conditioned knowledge of the senses and a re-learning of how to interpret them. Our attachments and beliefs can be obstacles in this process. Thus we turn to the senses with an equal measure of empathy and dispassion. We cultivate an approach that combines trust and open-mindedness with interrogation of self and the concepts by which we make sense of our experiences. If we are not derailed by our investments we gradually discover how to liberate the insights continually being offered by our senses from the conditioning that has come to define our relationship to the sensory realm.

At its core, this practice invites us to honour the constellation of body–mind–heart extending to it the kind of awareness we have in general become unaccustomed to doing. For instance, one frequently reads of individuals sustaining repeated stress injuries. These are usually the result of having persevered in an activity despite signs of bodily strain, even pain. Such evidence may have been ignored on account of the widespread conviction that there is no gain without pain. Concrete evidence of the body's challenge is overruled in favour of an abstract principle whose applicability is context-dependent and hardly universal. But the principle of 'no pain, no gain' likely affirms other ideas the injured individual may hold dear, such as the moral value of suffering or what counts as courage, fortitude, determination, an ideal body, etc. This ensemble then muffles the attempts of the senses to communicate, leading to an injury that could easily have been avoided. Learning to listen to the senses would involve confronting the entire web of ideas that mediates our relationship to self and world. The example offered here is a relatively simple one; but the process is the same even with complex phenomena like fear, anxiety or desire. None can be assumed to be self-evident; each invites the same investigative procedure. Over time communing with our senses becomes a reflexive practice, fluid, dynamic, ongoing.

Paying attention to the sensorium in this way makes it difficult to subscribe to an abstract notion of pleasure. We are simply too grounded in the concrete to be unaware of what we are required to dismiss, ignore or suppress when pleasure is construed as object and objective. In emphasising process this practice engenders its own temporality. It cannot be speeded up even though it does not by definition preclude speed as with the whirling dervish who embodies precisely such integrative awareness. To return to the senses is to settle for a tempo appropriate to honouring process. We are led to attend to the entire continuum of sensory experience not merely its extremes. The practice requires us to accept the limits of physicality, not as a negative constraint but as bounded potential. It opens us to the rich possibilities inherent in each moment, task, event or phenomenon. Each is understood not in discrete terms but as being the condensed, dispersed effect of past moments, tasks, events or phenomena; and as, in turn, initiating others yet to take shape or form.

Affirming the sensorium resists the predatory logic of an economy of pleasure in which hope and dissatisfaction are fatally intertwined. It sets aside the scorn for physicality at the heart of contemporary culture and enables us to experience integrated dynamism in everyday life. In doing so it leads us to discover that we have not been slaves to our senses as many have feared, so much as ensnared in a concept of pleasure disdainful of them.

ONCE UPON A TIME IN THE PRESENT

As a collectivity, humans suffer from a strange malady. It is one of our own making. Its symptoms are disaggregation, disarticulation, disequilibrium, dis-ease. The first two are the results of misperception. We have disaggregated things that are related to each other: humans and the rest of nature, mind–heart–body, self and all other 'isnesses'. In doing so, we have disarticulated their real relations proposing autonomy between things that are by their nature connected. The consequences of such misperception are disequilibrium and dis-ease. The former alludes to the resulting imbalance and inequity in the realms of economy, ecology, politics and society; the latter to the deficiencies and vulnerabilities — physical, emotional, mental — that undermine our individual and collective wellbeing. If proof of interconnectedness were ever required, it is evident in how the effects of cognitive disaggregation and disarticulation are materially manifest across a range of domains.

This fact should, in principle, discredit the notion that we can sequester, section, partition or isolate certain aspects of ourselves, our actions or our lives from the other dimensions with which they are inextricably bound. But it does not. This is because the truths of relationality are kept from being self-evident by miasmas which are both the cause and consequence of disaggregation and disarticulation. Still, their status as truths (as foundational principles whose functioning may be observed) means that they cannot be entirely exiled from our consciousness or experience. They hover around us, accompany us, and at times (especially of crisis) press upon us to emerge and see that which the miasma has been able to occlude but not eradicate. For it is the nature of truth to continually assert itself.

The potency or efficacy of a miasma is dependent on our allegiance to it. It is our enmeshment in, or attachment to, a given miasma that keeps us from noticing, and then appropriately synthesising, the evidence of our experience; not to mention its relation to the experience of others which, even when it differs from our own, calls upon us to reconsider our view. Such critical thinking is complicated by the fact that miasmas are by their nature illusions as well as delusions. As illusions miasmas lead us to see things that are not present and/or to fail to see things that are plainly there. In its delusory aspect miasmas can be so thoroughly internalised that they can seem logical and rational to one who subscribes to them. This is why information or evidence to the contrary can often fail to dislodge a miasmic way of seeing.

To speak of disaggregation is to presuppose a whole that is taken apart. In the process of being segmented, the importance of the whole to any sense-making endeavour is attenuated if not denied. This is so whether we are speaking of the whole in an explanatory or experiential sense. The segmented parts are then reordered and new relations between them proposed. Most frequently these new understandings suppose a hierarchy; they remake integral, reciprocal and horizontal relationships into a vertical system based on criteria that had not previously been considered salient as markers of otherness or differential value. This process alters our perception of the interrelations that actually pertain. This adds a further degree of obfuscation and often gives rise to secondary and tertiary miasmas in an effort to stabilise and fortify the initial misperception. Worse, it prepares the cognitive ground for normalising falsehood, violence and unethical action, invariable consequences of failing to grasp the real relations between things.

It is hoped that the preceding essays will have served to ground this more theoretical description, one recognisable to anyone who has reflected on the miasmas that shape contemporary thinking, among them, race, caste, gender, 'the free market'. The refusal to see how things are interwoven has led us to imagine life and politics as being about 'staking our claim upon the world'; not as we might see it were we to take the fact of interdependence and relationality to heart, as about 'taking our place in the world'. The former orients us to apprehending the world (nature, other human and non-human entities) as essentially external to us and existing for us. The latter inclines us toward perceiving our existence as one among countless 'isnesses' and admits the possibility of seeing each as equal and as equally endowed with sentience.

This view has long been embraced by mystics and tribal people and aspects of it have more recently found support among physicists and ecologists. To acknowledge this pre-history is not, however, to accept it wholesale. The recognition of all things as alive has evoked not merely tenderness, care and reverence for the natural world but also fear of it. This in turn has given rise to practices (some involving violence) intended to mollify spirits deemed angry or disturbed in order that their protection might be ensured. Our conviction of things as interconnected does not necessarily involve endorsing the problematic ways in which those interrelationships have previously been conceived.

II

In several essays we have looked to the etymology of words and to the meanings that have fallen into disuse to trace shifts in human perception. The exercise has illustrated how interrelations for which we may now need to argue were once taken for granted; indeed are compressed into the very structure of these terms and signalled by them. The obsolete meanings of words often intimate these prior understandings. I turn in the same spirit to examining the word 'conscience' and what its history may tell us about the way we have come to see our relationship to the world.

'Conscience' derives from the Latin *conscire*, from *con*, 'together' and *scire*, 'to know'. The *Oxford English Dictionary* lists its various meanings under three sections, two of which are relevant to my discussion. The first contains several obsolete meanings of conscience: inward knowledge or consciousness, internal conviction; internal or mental recognition or acknowledgement of something; knowledge, feeling, sense; inmost thought, mind, heart; reasonableness, understanding, 'sense'. This last meaning is noted as obsolete or rare.

The second section defines conscience as consciousness of right and wrong; moral sense. This meaning of conscience, more familiar in our day, is explained as: the internal acknowledgement or recognition of the moral quality of one's motives and actions; the sense of right and wrong as regards things for which one is responsible; the faculty or principle which pronounces upon the moral quality of one's actions or motives, approving the right and condemning the wrong.

What is immediately striking is the transformation of the meaning of conscience from inner knowledge, understanding, conviction, feeling and acknowledgement of something, to its current sense as being about the recognition of moral qualities, the faculty to judge right and wrong. Except for the fact that both meanings of conscience retain the idea of an inner sense, something known within oneself, the word would appear to have become something quite other than its original self. In a mutation analogous to what we observed in the case of aesthetics, we see a word that initially referred to knowledge or recognition of a thing and its properties ('acknowledgement of something') become instead a term about the human capacity for moral evaluation.

The transpersonal dimension of conscience as 'knowledge with or together' is diminished as the term overwhelmingly becomes identified with an individual's capacity for judging right from wrong and that too primarily in regards to her or his own motives and actions. As conscience meaning 'shared inner conviction' makes way for conscience understood as 'individual moral discernment' the term discards its relational aspect in several ways. Matters can henceforth be left to individual conscience as opposed to our conscience being itself a recognition and knowledge that we share with others as would have been the case before. Conscience becomes primarily about us, about our motives and actions.

What is more, evaluation emerges as an apparently autonomous process. It is independent of other humans. And also of the 'something' (whether human or non-human) that was previously being acknowledged, known, sensed and understood. The 'con' in conscience is weakened. What is more, the sense of conscience as relational knowledge, of being as much about the thing being recognised or acknowledged, is entirely missing. We go from a horizontal or coeval notion to a vertical, hierarchical one that privileges the consciousness of the one who judges.

The conceptual separation of the judge from the object of evaluation posits assessment as an abstract and fundamentally mental process. Unlike in the previous definition there is no longer a reference to the heart, to feeling, as being involved. The redefinition also implies that as a process judging can be deemed to be independent of the relationship between investigator and object of investigation. Furthermore, to the degree that conscience is deemed *moral faculty*, the capacity for judgement is emphasised over the way in which those judgements are arrived at. It follows from this that conscience can in principle be at work even without an understanding of that which is being judged right or wrong.

III

Did this transformation in the meaning of conscience presage the disaggregation of an integral view of things? Or was it, rather, its consequence? A social history of the term will be necessary to settle that issue. What we can say with some confidence is that here, as elsewhere, we witness a double displacement. A shared perspective of things as interrelated and having inherent meaning gives way to their being understood within a hierarchical evaluative schema which ascribes its own values. Second, even as this process reposes great faith in individual judgement it gradually weakens trust in the idea of collective knowledge. Indeed, the rise of the individual as moral arbiter and master interpreter renders the notion of knowing collectively a little suspect. It raises the spectre of a herd mentality with its connotations of an unreflective uniformity of thinking.

Some would be disconcerted by the idea that 'once there was wholeness and its fragmentation initiated disequilibrium'. It would invoke for them the Biblical fall from grace or any number of other cultural myths often premised on troubling notions of sin and redemption, crime and punishment. Also, in some theoretical quarters, wholeness has come to be understood as a deadening of difference, a suffocating sameness. Psychoanalysis, for example, conceives individuation as the effect of separation from a state of undifferentiatedness, a process often imagined as a moving out and away from wholeness. And post-structuralism has celebrated fragmentation as an inescapable dimension of life and labour in the contemporary period. Some of these latter concerns, as I have argued earlier, are antithetical responses to dissatisfaction with the way in which wholeness has been conceived.

As for the anxiety regarding 'fall from grace narratives' it should, I hope, be clear that I am not in these essays presenting a moral fable of our brokenness as a species. Rather, I am attempting to trace elements of the story of how the failure to see our mutuality, equality and relatedness to all forms of life makes us seriously deluded about the nature of our existence. This in turn prepares the ground for the kinds of carelessness, violence and indifference toward self and other 'isnesses' that is so evident today. We have widely misperceived the real relations between things, between causes and their effects. These misrecognitions have become normative. This poses a crisis not merely of knowledge but also of morality, that is to say, of how to live. For understanding causality is crucial to developing an ethics, to learning how we might take our place in the world, not merely stake our claim upon it.

ON DAYS LIKE THIS

On days like this
it is hard to pretend to normalcy
to not kiss the earth in gratitude
The interwovenness of things is so palpable
that the body is alive with the knowledge of it
It seems unfathomable why this truth so plainly felt
can seem abstract to anyone
Yet, it is no mystery really
for everything conspires to undermine our perception of it
Systems of learning carve infinity into byte-sized morsels
each in their own way
and train our gaze on what they identify as worthy
Narrowing our focus
at times scattering our attention
Making it difficult to notice
this elementary fact
about the world in which we live

AFTERWORD

In following a story, we follow a storyteller, or, more precisely, we follow the trajectory of a storyteller's attention ... It's like following a dance, not with our feet and bodies, but with our observation and our expectations and our memories of lived life.[1]

These essays have traced some threads in the tapestry of the present. In them I have striven to share the trajectory of my attention. The question of what prevents us from recognising our interdependent mutuality has been a lifelong concern (though I would not have phrased it in this way earlier). It led me to Marxism, to feminism and thence to cultural studies. The bequest of each is evident in this book, even though feminism is admittedly an absent presence, discernible in the interest in bodies, process, feeling, in experience as a basis for knowing.

The discovery of the sacred in the midst of a catastrophic illness, the life of the spirit to which I was unexpectedly called and was irresistibly drawn, shattered the way I had hitherto made sense of things. Internally, I felt no contradiction between the core impulses of Marxism and feminism and the direction in which I seemed to be travelling. I instinctively sensed the potential for widening and deepening the concerns of both. To follow the altered arc of my attention seemed to me to honour the true spirit of each.

The journey has led me to recast the frame as well as the terms of my engagement with the world. For example, concern with social inequality broadened to include a root precondition, the absence of a feeling of our interwovenness. In the simultaneously inward and outward dynamic of contemplation, this gradually extended to exploring the absence of that same mutuality vis-à-vis the self, for instance, in the relations of mind, body and heart (something to which feminism had pointed in its own way). It was only natural for this to slowly transpose itself into the more general question of how we had come to disaggregate things that were interconnected; then to ponder its implications not just for dominant ideologies but also for those perspectives that had set out to challenge them.

This description formalises as though it were linear, a process that was far more chaotic and recursive. For even when clarity was glimpsed, or sensed, understanding emerged only gradually, and the language for conveying it was slower still in arriving. It was as though the kaleidoscope of perception was slowly being turned, suggesting new patterns and affiliations. Questions not previously considered came to the fore and older ones proposed themselves within a new constellation of concerns. My secular analytical lexicon (Marxist, feminist, poststructuralist) had to be supplemented with understandings and concepts from spiritual traditions (among others, dependent co-arising, the sentience of matter, the materiality of the so-called non-material such as thought or feeling, the indivisibility of the 'physical' and 'metaphysical').

In sharing these details I extend a commitment to process that was integral to my own learning. It was by means of such continual attention that I was able to grasp the violence that indifference to process makes normative. I knew this intellectually; but the understanding of it yielded by the practice of mindfulness was of an altogether different order. This discipline made it impossible to imagine violence as existing only 'out there', to not also become attuned to the violence one routinely (if unwittingly) practised toward one's own self or others, which in its capacity to wound and distort was like any unleashed by structures deemed external. Inner *vs* outer, Self *vs* Other, thought *vs* deed, mind *vs* body, knowledge *vs* devotion, art *vs* craft, humans *vs* the rest of nature, sacred *vs* secular: every opposition revealed itself as the effect of conditioned perception, a failure to comprehend the multiple webs of interrelations in which all things (temporarily) assumed shape, texture and solidity.

The feminist concept of intersectionality had come closest to getting at this. But 'intersection' suggested something rather different than 'interwoven'. It seemed to indicate areas of overlap but retained a degree of separateness and fixity so far as the categories of analysis were concerned. It also did not sufficiently disrupt the notion of difference as division. This meant that difference in its sense as specificity could easily cede ground to the idea of difference as otherness. Such a conception militates against a unitive approach; one which addresses contradictions and unequal relations without ever losing hold of what is shared, of our inextricability.

The expanding scope of my own interests urged me towards a different formulation: to conceive of division as the effect of socially-produced misperception, and of difference as the play of specificity within interdependent diversity. This seemed to offer a way of addressing at once, the social basis of all perceived divisions, the rich particularity of phenomena, and their interconnectedness within an indivisible whole. 'The whole' indicated the potentially infinite interrelations of matter and energy in which all things existed. It was understood as being too vast to be mapped analytically. But acknowledging it initiated a profound reorientation in how one thought about the interrelations of particulars in any, necessarily partial, investigation.

As new terms of inquiry took shape one was enabled to return to classic cultural studies concerns (questions of power, ideology, knowledge, everyday life) and objects of study (market rationale, advertising, urban planning, political discourse) but in a way that it may not have been inclined to, or that went beyond its customary focus. And alongside this to pursue, as I have here, issues with which it has not engaged. It is thus that some essays are identifiably cultural studies in their approach and others are not.

Since this collection reflects on the present, the question of disaggregated thinking and practice has been addressed principally in relation to the logic of the market. The problem precedes modernity as the *longue durée* of gender and caste discrimination reminds us. But disaggregation took a quantum leap with industrialisation, and another with the technological advancements that have made possible the current phase of globalised production and consumption. In every way, and at every turn, we are continually required to think and act in ways that evade, overlook and deny the fact of interwovenness, to slice, dice, separate and segregate that which is integrally related. This propensity has made credible the obfuscation of cause-effect relations and contributed to the normalisation of violence and the ethical breakdown that it enables.

To insist on re-aggregating is to resist this paradigm. Attention to process and an integrated awareness of the sensorium are important to such an effort. What might this mean? In relation to the internet, for instance, it could involve developing a culture of use that conserves focus and resists distraction through continual attention to body, mind and heart when one is online. It may also include deliberately opting for slower internet connections and download speeds, pausing to take a deep breath before clicking on a hyperlink, making each click a considered decision, and adopting other strategies so as to proceed in awareness, rather than simply be carried along by the currents of speed, simultaneity and multiplicity. The idea would be to engage technology in a way that disrupts the logic of its current design. Where ethical hacking and Open Source software undermine the commercial and proprietary basis of the internet, mindful internet practices can challenge a default mode of engagement, with its corrosive effects and diminishing returns. The slowing down that is intrinsic to mindfulness tends to lead one in a thoughtful direction, away from the frenzy that feeds the spiral of aspiration and hyperconsumption on which the market economy in this period crucially depends.

A key argument in this book is that the issues we confront require us to move beyond antithesis, to reach for a new theoretical and political synthesis. Many of our debates are framed narrowly, in binary terms insufficient to the problems at hand. The question of free speech is a case in point. It tends to be a duel between those in favour of making speech conditional (in certain circumstances, in relation to certain subjects) and those against such censorship on grounds that free expression is a democratic right. It is difficult to disagree with the latter position. But is it always sufficient as a response? Why not simultaneously address the question of 'right speech' when relevant? Doing so would draw attention to complex issues at times improperly, or else unsatisfactorily, condensed into the notion of 'offence'. It would require us to think through difficult questions of intent, context, consequence, mode of expression, to elaborate an ethic of speech distinct from the claims of those using offence to silence and discipline. An abstract defence of rights without a concomitant consideration of these matters increasingly fails to convince. Indifference to consequence is a stratagem of power today. When resistance or critique evinces a similar disregard it does so at its own peril.

The imagination of critique is shaped by the modalities of power in a given period: what it affirms, denies, evades, insists upon, pretends is untrue. I hope these essays will have struck a chord with readers' 'observation[s], expectations and . . . memories of lived life';[2] that we can agree that we are called upon to reclaim life in a way that is matter-loving, sentience-affirming and process-honouring. If we did, capitalism could not long survive. Relatedly, we need to countenance the idea of limits, whether in relation to ourselves or to market-driven economic growth. Acting as though there are none has created suffering, destroyed bodies, societies, the quality of life. To embrace limits would be to set aside the miasma of a freedom from constraint. The idea of bounded potential serves us better.

Bounded potential suggests dynamism within a circumference. It locates us in a 'someplace'. But also relationally; our potential is related to our being bound together. One may even say it points to our potential as being intrinsically tied to our interdependencies. It is not a human-centric notion; it pertains equally to the rest of nature. It can accommodate the determinate, the mysterious, the unpredictable and the uncontrollable in the unfolding of individual and collective potential. It precludes hubris. The idea of bounded potential runs counter to all that has brought us to the crisis we currently face. It is an orientation to self, life and world that renews and restores.

Notes

1. John Berger, *Bento's Sketchbook*, London: Verso, 2011, p. 72.
2, Ibid.

GLOSSARY

adharma	living in a manner that contravenes dharma
bhajan	devotional song
bhajan mandali	group that sings *bhajans* (devotional songs)
chappal	Indian slippers
dharma	term grounded in Hindu-Buddhist religio-spiritual framework, often translated as law, duty, right conduct. In this text designates living and acting on the basis of the interdependence and radical equality of all life forms
dhoti	traditional male attire, a rectangular piece of cloth wrapped around the waist
gulal	coloured powder used to celebrate the spring festival, Holi
gullies	narrow lanes
guru	spiritual teacher

'isness'	the specific quality and expression of sentience or aliveness manifested by a person or thing
jalebi wallah	seller of jalebis, a deep fried sweet
kadai	wok
kumkum	vermillion powder used in Hindu rituals and applied by Hindu women on their foreheads as adornment
kurta	loose-fitting shirt
masala	spices
mullah	Muslim priest
pavement	sidewalk
puja	worship
pyjama	loose-fitting pant
rajas	activity
rasa	literally juice or essence; feelings evoked by aesthetic practices and forms
riyaz	music practice
salwar kameez	tunic-like top worn over loose-fitting pants by women
sattva	alert stillness
shambrani	frankincense
tamas	inertia
tempos	small vehicles for transporting goods

ABOUT THE AUTHOR

Lata Mani is a feminist historian and cultural critic. She started her working career in media planning, but her involvement with the women's movement inspired her to abandon it for graduate school. She completed an MA in Comparative World History (1983) and a doctoral degree in History of Consciousness (1989) at the University of California, Santa Cruz. She joined the faculty in Women's Studies at the University of California, Davis in 1990. She held this position until a head injury she sustained in an automobile accident in 1993 inaugurated a new intellectual phase that continues to provide grist for the mill of her writing and analysis.

She has published in the areas of modern Indian history, feminism, spiritual philosophy, and contemporary politics and culture. She is the author of *Contentious Traditions: The Debate on Sati in Colonial India* (1998); *SacredSecular: Contemplative Cultural Critique* (2009); and *Interleaves: Ruminations on Illness and Spiritual Life* (2011). She also collaborated with Ruth Frankenberg in compiling, 'The Tantra Chronicles', published online. Her academic essays have appeared in *Cultural Critique, Cultural Studies, Economic and Political Weekly, Economy and Society, Feminist Review*, and *Seminar*.

CPSIA information can be obtained
at www.ICGtesting.com
Printed in the USA
BVHW042149280819
557112BV00010B/135/P

9 780415 831383